PRAISE FOR *WIN THE JOB YOU WANT!*

"[*Win the Job You Want!*] is well-done and I believe anyone in a job search can benefit from using it. It is an easy read with a focused approach to the various aspects of a job search and how to pursue each action. The organization is logical and positive with emphasis on self-analysis and self-help while not ignoring family, friends and others impacted by the situation.

There are numerous analogies throughout that use familiar settings or circumstances to illustrate the current point of discussion. This brings the thought process "up close and personal" for ease of understanding. Additionally, the job seeker's thought process is continually broken down into manageable "bite-size" pieces in multi-step approaches to organized analysis and attack of each feature of the search.

This book offers a common sense approach to the specifics of a job search but also provides the individual with skills that have a direct translation to day-to-day performance in the new job."

—*JH, U.S. Military*

"Am very impressed [with *Win the Job You Want!*]. It is well organized and written. I especially liked the time spent on the emotional issues, which often are the candidate's greatest enemy. I can't tell you how many times I have counseled a new job-seeker to 'get over it... ok, you got screwed, now let's talk about what you can do for your next employer.' A couple months ago I had such a conversation with a very senior guy who just wouldn't let go. I finally gave up trying to convince him otherwise!

I also liked the summary section of each chapter. I think the book is a refreshing perspective for the job seeker in today's environment."

—*RM, Professional Recruiter*

"It's concise, easy to follow, and packed with useful information."

—*GB, Non-profit*

"Very understandable. Inviting to read. The more you read the more you want to read. Secrets 4 and 5 were most helpful and I learned the most I didn't know. The bonus on job fit: I thought I knew this, but didn't!"

—RC, *Transportation (Job seeker)*

"Really liked it a lot. Easy to read, full of clear, detailed examples of "dos" and "don'ts." It takes you through the whole process. And it's so pragmatic! I especially like the "don'ts"—that is something people should really take to heart. And the reminder to be kind and respectful to everyone you meet along the job seeking process. I know more than one candidate who got 'dissed' by an assistant for rudeness. Now there's a real deal-breaker."

—MK, *Non-profit*

Thank you for the copy of your book. I was only able to look at it briefly on Sun. night before my interview, so I went to some specific topics first. I found the information and ideas quite helpful—especially the part on possible questions to be prepared for. And sure enough the interviewer yesterday asked versions of both of them—the one about where I want to be in 5 years and what my weaknesses are. Thanks to reading those pages the very day before, I had some thought out answers. And now I plan to read your book properly, from start to end.

—AP, *Engineering (Job Seeker)*

WIN THE JOB YOU WANT!

7 SECRETS

HIRING MANAGERS DON'T TELL YOU.

 *But we will!*

PAT ANDREW & ELEANOR HILL

HIGHERLIFE
DEVELOPMENT SERVICES, INC
Oviedo, Florida

Win the Job You Want!
By Patricia A. Andrew and Eleanor A. Hill
Copyright © 2012 by Patricia A. Andrew and Eleanor A. Hill

Authors' note: Throughout this book and our other products we use "him," "he," and other masculine pronouns when writing about Hiring Managers. This is purely for ease of reading and to avoid the awkwardness of "s/he," "him/her," etc. as we certainly know and appreciate the fact that today, there are probably as many female Hiring Managers as there are male Hiring Managers.

ISBN: 978-1-935245-62-9
Published by HigherLife Publishing and Marketing

www.TheCareerSuite.com

Printed in the United States of America.

For the over 24 million unemployed or underemployed in America and all those around the world who deserve better.

TABLE OF CONTENTS

Contents

ACKNOWLEDGEMENTS

According to Winston Churchill, writing a book comes in four stages. It begins as a toy or novelty, but by stage four, it has become a tyrant, ruling your life. If Churchill was right, then this book has been the exception to that "rule" and for that we give credit and appreciation to all the outstanding Hiring Managers who helped us to make this book a reality.

We could fill a book with just the names of all the Hiring Managers we consulted! Each Hiring Manager was gifted, passionate, and placed a high value on the information he or she shared freely within these pages to job seekers everywhere. As a whole, they recognized that a book like this has the ability to streamline the entire hiring process, so that parties from both sides of the desk can walk away satisfied with a successful, comprehensive experience.

In short, we've done the "grunt work" for you. We called, e-mailed, and visited Hiring Managers that we knew in an effort to expand our reach and provide you with the most comprehensive, accurate information on what Hiring Managers want to see in job candidates.

Responses quickly arrived from various industries and professional disciplines throughout the United States. People like: Blaine Sweatt, John Caron, and John Ruggieri—all senior leaders, highly experienced Hiring Managers, and builders of effective and successful teams. Sarah Jackson, Jack Snow, Tami Kaiser, and Dan Lyons in human resource leadership and Mike Clawson from consumer products marketing all added valuable insights.

We also heard from Ken Grover, who has a perspective on law enforcement and loss prevention, and Bill Herzig from international supply chain. Michael Sampson added his insights from the legal arena, and Jim Ireland and Margot H. Knight from non-profit organizations.

From defense contracting, we spoke with Joy Sabol and Kathy Arce. From finance, the contributors included Margaret Grayson, Rick

Cardenas, Jim Gase, Steve Helsel, Jean Williams, and Steve Wenner-strom. Recruiters and executive search process professionals, who responded to our questions, included Andy Steinem, Jack Groban, Dr. Robert Bender, Dick Maglio, Barbara Wiley, and Bruce Thibodeau.

We also heard from people in hospitality, consumer foods, arts and culture, public accounting, manufacturing, government, publishing, international business, compensation and benefits, consulting, training and development, banking, commercial fishing, and retail management.

Their heartfelt respect for this project was matched only by their wisdom, kindness, competence, and patience. We thank each of them for generously sharing their time and their phenomenal insights on job search success.

Last, but not least, we also thank countless others who have read and critiqued this book and enriched the final product for the benefit of job seekers everywhere.

PREFACE

A story is told about a man who was on his way to celebrate an important event when he fell into a deep pit with steep, slippery walls. He tried to escape again and again and despaired over the thought that he could never get out. He saw the daylight above him, but just couldn't climb up to it on his own. He decided to call out for help.

After several hours, various acquaintances and colleagues passing by heard his call for help. One by one, each looked into the pit and offered him advice, even tossed him some tools, and each one encouraged him not to give up.

Some of the advice was genuinely worthwhile. The various tools they gave him helped somewhat. With their encouragement and the tools they tossed to him, he was able to climb part of the way up, but always slipped back down. He tried again and again, but nothing helped him to reach the top.

He became more and more discouraged. The situation, indeed, looked bleak.

Then two friends came upon the pit and heard him calling for help. They stopped and called down to him. He looked up with a wan smile of recognition, but by this time, had almost given up. Then to his amazement and horror, both these friends jumped down into the pit with him.

Dumbfounded, he cried, "Why did you do that? Now we're all in the pit!"

"Yes," said one friend, "but we know the way out." And sure enough, within moments, they showed him the way, and all three were quickly out of the pit. The man expressed much appreciation and then continued on his way to the celebration.

If you are one of the more than 24 million unemployed or underemployed in America, it's our desire to "jump down into the pit" with you! That's because we've been where you are—a few times. And we know the way out.

We feel your pain and we know you deserve better. We know it's important to not only find a job, but to engage in the kind of work that will give you true job satisfaction.

There's nothing magic about what you'll discover within the pages of this book. A lot of it is common sense. But when we are under the stress of losing a job and in a hurry to find another, we tend to react without thinking. This book provides the tools to help replace a panicked reaction with a thoughtfully planned response that will lift you out of the pit of unemployment quickly and with less stress on you and your family.

We include your family in this equation because we recognize that it's not just you your unemployment affects. It's you and everyone who cares about you and everyone you care about.

The book you are holding is a compilation of interviews with Hiring Managers from various industries all across America, as well as our own 30 years of combined managing and marketing consulting, human resources management and leadership development experience. We are ready to share our knowledge with you and help you get the job you want.

Know this: We *can* do it together. You *can* win the job you want—now.

Pat Andrew   Eleanor Hill

INTRODUCTION

Most books on this subject spend pages telling you the distressing news:

- The economy is bad.

- The stock market is unstable (when isn't it).

- The national debt is growing out of control.

- One financial meltdown after another is forcing good, skilled, highly qualified people out of their jobs.

- The overall fallout is runaway credit card debt, foreclosures on homes and retirements delayed.

- Unemployment, in some regions, still hovers at 15 percent and higher.

Yes, you hear about this from everyone, everywhere. So, we're not going to spend any more time or words about this than what you see in the above bulleted list.

When we hear all of these "bad news bears" on a day-to-day basis, we can become mentally and emotionally paralyzed by continuing to focus only on what can stop you from getting the job you want. In this book, we want you to turn your thoughts and energies to *what can help you; the positive steps that help you forge ahead to get that job quickly.* Yes, even in this kind of depressed job market.

Don't get us wrong, we're not going to tell you to stick your head in the sand and overlook the current financial crisis—it's definitely a factor; but it is not the only factor and there are helpful steps you can take to overcome those potential roadblocks in your quest to find a new job. So if you feel like you've fallen into that slippery pit—you don't have to stay there. Let us show you the way out!

PREPARE YOURSELF PERSONALLY AND FINANCIALLY FOR SUCCESS

You Can Land the Job You Want—Now

You don't have to accept being unemployed or settle for being under-employed. **Every company is hiring people who can offer precisely what they need, when they need it.** This book's purpose is to coach you in how to stand out from the crowd of other job seekers and land the job you want—now.

Do you have what it takes to land your dream job? If you want a great job, you will need:

No one lacks confidence. That is a fallacy. You either have confidence that you can do (or be) something or you have confidence that you cannot! So remember: success comes in "cans," not in "cannots."

- A strong, disciplined mind set.
- Marketing know-how.
- Sustained energy.
- A highly motivated confidence.
- To know what the Hiring Manager and his company need.
- To present yourself to that Hiring Manager as the uniquely qualified candidate to fulfill those needs.

Feeling overwhelmed? Don't. We'll show you how in simple, easy-to-follow steps in this book.

Success Story

Did you ever see someone just destroy themselves playing tennis, golf, or even in a business meeting because they became so frustrated or despondent about themselves or their performance? They began losing, didn't they? Well, that was Jackson during the first weeks of his job search.

Jackson was still angry about being fired. When anyone asked him how his job search was going he was defensive and confused. He was concerned about all the money he and his family were spending with very little coming in. After a time, Jackson had a difficult time just getting out of bed in the morning, let alone putting forth his best effort during interviews.

One day, he asked a friend for an introduction to a company where he really wanted to work. The friend (and he certainly was a friend!) told him that as much as he liked Jackson, he couldn't do it. Stunned, Jackson snorted, "Why not?"

His friend answered, "Listen to yourself! Look at yourself in the mirror. You look and sound so negative. You're better than this, but no one—and especially an interviewer—will see or hear it, or consider hiring you. Get your act together and then we'll talk about making some introductions."

While driving home, Jackson kept playing his friends words over in his mind again and again. What hit him the most was that his friend knew "he was better than this." Jackson wanted to believe this. And he knew he had to gain control of himself to really see it and succeed in his job search.

The first thing he did was to make a list of all the negative thoughts and emotions he had been experiencing. Then, he began replacing them with positive ones. Yes, some negative thoughts would still nag at him. But now, he stopped reacting and started to put into practice what he was learning. He also was genuinely grateful when his family and friends did and said things to support him.

It took discipline and courage, but as he did this, he saw great changes. A great change occurred in his relationship with his family as they all pulled together to develop a financial budget to last them through Jackson's job search.

And, you guessed it, the next time he saw his friend, Jackson smiled broadly saying, "Even if you don't introduce me to (name withheld), you've done a world of good for me, and I truly thank you." His friend returned the smile and said, "Now, let me do even more—let me make that introduction!"

Remember: It's important to recognize that your decisions master you. And it's up to you—and only you—to make the decisions that help you. Don't let anyone tell you that you cannot control your thoughts and emotions. If that's how they feel, well, that's their decision and you don't have to accept it. So don't!

PREPARE YOURSELF PERSONALLY TO WIN IN TODAY'S HYPER-COMPETITIVE JOB MARKET

It is crucial to prepare your thoughts, emotions, and spirit—in essence, shore them up—so that you will be both sustained and successful during the rigors of a job search. If you are not ready, the task can overwhelm. However, if you *are* ready and have a plan, you view the task differently and this makes the task more manageable, less stressful, and even enjoyable.

Who and What Is a "Hiring Manager"

You may be asking: "Who and what are these Hiring Managers?" Well, they're the people who:

1. Have a current or near future need to hire someone to fill a job.

2. Have the authority and responsibility to decide who gets that job.

For the most part, these Hiring Managers are middle to upper management in business functions such as operations, information technology, finance, legal, marketing & sales, human resources, chief executive level management, and other similar roles.

Human resource (HR) staff sometimes act as the Hiring Manager and often manage the hiring process. We included their input here as well.

Finally, the Hiring Managers we interviewed all have a *minimum* of five years experience in their positions, so they are highly qualified to respond to and provide relevant, insightful answers to the questions we asked in our interviews. They are the people you'd want to get advice from and to have as a mentor throughout your job search process—*if you could*. And *now, you can*, within the pages of this book.

Buzz Words from Hiring Managers

Hiring Managers, in various industries all across the United States, told us how important it is for job seekers to be prepared mentally and emotionally before they interview with their companies for a job. The Hiring Manager will always look for an employee who is knowledgeable, skilled, and accomplished in their field of work.

In describing such people, they also stressed words and phrases like:

- *Enthusiasm*
- *Genuine*
- *Confident*
- *Interacts Positively*
- *Focused and Energized*
- *Sense of Passion*
- *Genuine Curiosity*
- *Solid*
- *Optimistic*
- *Sincere*
- *Friendly*
- *A "Fire in the Belly"*

So what exactly do we mean when we speak of preparing your thoughts, emotions and spirit? Thoughts and emotions are pretty up front. It's pretty well established that how and what you think can impact how you feel (your emotions) and how you feel can make a difference in how you act.

"Spirit" is not mystical or religious in the job search context. It relates to your inner strength, courage, integrity, and conviction. It's what lifts your thought and emotions off the emotional roller coaster of a job search. Your spirit is the part of you that enhances your power to maintain a sense of calm assurance and increases the effectiveness of your actions over the long run.

The right mind set, emotions, and inner spirit are a solid foundation upon which to build the framework of a successful job search marketing plan.

So, Take a Breath, then Let It Go

Don't panic. Panic paralyzes your thinking and drains your energy. It freezes you in the past. The only way anyone can move toward a better future is to look with enthusiasm and hope toward that future. When you are seeking new employment, it is more important than ever to stay open to the possibilities.

There are scores of job openings for people who can prove themselves to be of value to a potential employer. Claim this truth for yourself and hold fast to it:

I am one of the problem-solvers that employers need right now.

A new employer will never recognize your value if you are angry, discouraged, or depressed. *But,* they definitely will recognize your potential value to them when you show confidence, enthusiasm and a sincere desire to help them.

The Good News Is That:

- **You can control and rid yourself of negative thoughts and emotions** by replacing them with positive emotions that will act as a spotlight for the value you have to offer. This is where your spirit of courage and conviction enter the picture.

    Should depression or other such emotions intrude on your day, talk to yourself (use self-speak) or talk to a professional. Do something good for yourself. Concentrate on the good in your life. And remember to be grateful for and to thank someone who has shown you support. In any case, do not allow negative emotions to drag on and drag you down.

Someone once said, "If we allow the serpent of negativity to drag on in our lives, it becomes a dragon that turns on us." A silly play on words? Not so, friend. It's a rule to thrive by. So, make your choice. Wouldn't you rather take on a small serpent than some fire-breathing, havoc-wreaking dragon? That's got to be a no-brainer.

- Whether you believe it or not, losing a job is *not* the end of the world. It is simply a form of change; and it's what you make of that change that makes the difference in your outcome. In fact, when viewed correctly, this change can be a beginning of a more satisfying, enriching work life. Just don't get caught in the anger, blame and even denial that keep you looking backward instead of forward.

Change Always Begins and Ends With What You Make of It

In other words, whether change is useful and stabilizing in your life or harmful and disruptive depends on you and whether you *respond* to it or *react* to it. Again, this is where your spirit or inner strength sustains you.

Used in this context, *respond* means "to answer another's words or actions to one's own advantage." *React*, on the other hand, means "to answer another's words or actions to one's own disadvantage."

There is nothing a Hiring Manager wants more than a problem-solver and nothing he wants less than a "wallower."

When you respond, you give yourself an opportunity to solve the problem. If you react, you only give yourself an opportunity to wallow in the problem. You become part of the problem and no one ever solved a problem by becoming part of it.

You can think of "wallow" as a contraction of "we allow." That's because the more *we allow* ourselves to focus on the negative things in our past, the more they dominate us and cause us to *wallow* in them, to the detriment of the present and future good in our lives. So, don't wallow!

Reach deep inside to your inner strength and you'll maintain a stable emotional level. That means not too high (when things are going well) or too low (when they aren't). Recognize that you will have emotional ups and downs. This is normal. But they don't have to be extreme or erratic, if you bring balance to your thinking and emotions.

Employ Some of These "Self-speak" Suggestions and Say Them Often to Yourself

- "Being between jobs doesn't define me. I am a capable and valuable addition to a company. What took place in the past is past. I'm simply in a transition period between a previous good job and a future good job—that's all!"

- "I am completely able to master the challenge of finding a job and will engage in the 'adventure' and enjoy it. Others will notice."

- "I am not impressed by scary employment or economic statistics. I know there are job opportunities for the kind of problem-solver I am. My energy, enthusiasm, confidence, experience, and selling ability will make a positive difference for me during my job search."

- "I will get a job! Even if I don't know immediately how or when, I know it will improve for me, and I look forward to the search process."

Employ Some of These Action Steps to Stay on the Right Track

- Make your job search your full-time (albeit short-term) job, but take time off when you've earned it and give yourself a pat on the back.

- Set short-term, concrete, meaningful goals for your job search and reward yourself for those achievements.

- Designate someone to call upon and talk to regularly about your search and your feelings. Keep in touch with others and don't isolate yourself.

- Write down, or make a mental list, on a regular basis, all the things and people you are grateful for.

- Exercise more than usual to vent any frustrations and to help keep your thoughts about yourself up and energized.

- Take time to thank the people who help you during your job search.

Now, we are not saying that you will never experience or express the various emotions associated with change. Emotional feelings of sadness, fear, denial, anger, and even shock are normal. What we are saying is that it is not what you feel as much as how you deal with these emotions that is important. Whether you *respond* or *react*. Whether you help yourself or hurt yourself.

The information in this book and all the useful materials that you'll find at our website, www.TheCareerSuitecom, are designed to help you help yourself.

So, let's put change to work for you instead of against you—step-by-step.

FIRST: STOP LOOKING BACK AND MOVE FORWARD

Have you ever attempted to drive a car forward by only looking through the rear view mirror or out the back window? You might be able to do it if there are no turns to make or obstacles to avoid or people entering your path. Even if the road is straight and there are no obstacles in your way, how far do you think you'd get before you run off the road looking only through your back window? As they say on television, don't try this at home!

The only way to successfully drive forward is to look forward—to look where you're going, not just where you've been. Look in your job "rearview mirror" only to access and preserve valuable relationships and experiences from the past. Then, turn your whole experience with any previous employer into useful "lessons learned." Use those lessons to *pave* the way forward to a new job.

The Problem and Solution

There are five stages of transition that people generally go through when they experience change that necessitates turning away from the past and looking forward. If you've lost your job, you are experiencing one or more of these right now. Before delving into each of these stages, consider the following analogy:

Each stage of transition is like a vestibule in a house. The purpose of a vestibule is to take off unneeded coats, etc. before entering the home. You don't hang out in the vestibule and complain about why you took off your coat. You quickly hang up your coat and proceed into the home. Why? Because that is where you want to be. That's where the fun is and the sense of well-being.

The same goes for the transition stages. Consider them to be the vestibule to your new job. Move as quickly as possible through them; put them behind you as you progress into your job search activities. This will keep you focused on where you want to be ("at home" with a new employer) and to get you there as quickly as possible.

When we discuss each stage, we have included what is generally the main problem associated with that stage. In addition, we provide you with a possible solution (or response) to help lift you out of the quicksand and place you on solid ground.

You may want to copy these problems and solutions on separate three by five cards and keep them with you. Highlight the solution. Refer to them when you feel you're about to get on the emotional roller coaster associated with a transition stage and focus on being responsive, not reactive. It will keep you on the right path to success and out of the snares that would trap you in delay and missed opportunities.

Ask yourself: "Where am I in this change process today?" Look forward and implement the solution. Don't waste your time and energy by allowing yourself to get stuck in unproductive, distracting emotions. Remember, one definition of insanity is doing the same thing you've always done the same way you've always done it expecting to get different results. To begin something new, you generally have to stop doing something old. The old is the problem. The new is the solution. Go to it!

1. Denial/Disbelief

The problem: This can't be happening to me! This shock will wear off.

The solution: Focus forward. Be grateful for the good you have experienced. Gratitude for even the smallest good keeps you positively focused and moving forward.

2. Anger

The problem: Why me? I'll show them or I'll get even. I've been unfairly wronged.

The solution: Remember, anger is a boomerang and "the best revenge is living well!" So, get on with your success and leave the disappointments behind. Try to sincerely forgive the people involved. Anger does nothing to whom or whatever is causing the anger, but it keeps you in a weakened, unproductive, and agitated state of mind.

3. Blame

The problem: It's not my fault, so and so is to blame. Focusing on blame will only keep you in the past. Rehearsing the "wrong"—real or imagined—only hurts you, not them, and it could cause you to lose your next job even before you get it!

The solution: Recognize and accept that the past is the past. Acknowledge that you've got a great future ahead of you. Give it your full and undivided attention and participation!

4. Discouragement or Even Depression

The problem: Feelings of hopelessness, loss, shame, frustration, bitterness, isolation, out of control, numb.

The solution: Stay connected with people, create a routine for yourself that you can joyfully anticipate, and take one day at a time. The opposite of discouragement is *courage*. Gather your courage on your own and with help. Develop a plan; start working it. Get professional help. Don't procrastinate—*do it now*! You have a great life to live; get on with it.

5. Acceptance

The problem: Many people think of this as resignation. It's not. Resignation is stagnation or giving in. Don't be resigned to not having a job.

The solution: *Accept the fact that this is merely a change in your life and move on.* Accept the fact that you already have a new job: you're the CEO, for heaven's sake, of your own job search. Accept that there is greater opportunity ahead of you. Seek it or create it! This is your time for thinking of positive possibilities, personal growth, a new birth of enthusiasm for your life and your work.

SECOND: ASK FOR AND ENCOURAGE SUPPORT FROM YOUR FAMILY AND FRIENDS

Even when you do look forward, you may need some additional help. How about a map or other directions to guide you to what may be an unknown destination? What about a navigator to watch for road signs and to help you find the right road or address? What about enthusiasm for the trip and confidence in your ability to make it? What about some encouragement from your family and friends as you proceed? Would these be helpful? You bet! The same is true as you prepare for and proceed with your job search. Especially then! So, be sure to keep your family (and friends) engaged and informed when possible.

It's fairly obvious that your family will be affected by your job change. They need and like to be kept up to date on what's happening. So be open and honest with them. Let them know that you're approaching your "new job" of heading your own job search as a professional. Explain how you're marketing yourself to companies you are interested in. Ask for their help in researching these companies and in building a referral network, and include them in your decision-making process. Recognize and appreciate the fact that they

Job Seekers need a strong support team of family and friends. Ask for their help in researching and networking.

will want to help you move through this change process. Allow them to do so because it will help both you and them.

Make financial plans together with your spouse or life-partner. Examine your financial situation honestly and realistically. Gain his or her commitment to work together. If you have children, present a united front both to involve them and to inform them. Let your children know that you want them to be part of the decision-making process, when appropriate, but that you and your spouse or life-partner will be making the big decisions. If they are old enough, ask them to be your sounding board for your ideas and ask them for their ideas as well.

At all times, if possible, maintain your optimism and show your family you are moving in a positive direction and that you expect good results in a timely fashion. Remember, you want and need their support and they need yours.

If you have children, they will sense that something is different and will be curious. In a recent ABC Network poll, thirty-six percent of job seekers with children saw a change in them; for those unemployed six months or more, seventy-five percent saw a change in their children.

If you don't tell them what's happening, they may even think whatever's happening is their fault. Don't refrain from telling them—openly and honestly. They are more resilient than you might think and will probably react to the situation better than you expect. In any case, they need to feel loved and secure.

They need to be included when it is appropriate; ask them to pick up some slack in chores and financial adjustments. They need to know that although you'll accept input about the financial adjustments that affect them, they are not the final decision-makers on what those financial adjustments will be.

In addition, they don't need to know the details of the loss of your previous job, nor should you vent or display anger towards your previous employer in front of them. Simply deal with their concerns calmly and sincerely and show them you are optimistic and are moving forward to find a new job.

For your own peace of mind, remember: the scoreboard may show you behind, but there is nothing like encouragement from the crowd (your family or support team) to bring about the turning point that leads to victory. Having and acknowledging the value of their support will help both you and them cope and minimize the amount of stress involved for all concerned.

Ideas to Draw the Family Together—Turn this into an Opportunity to Strengthen your Bonds

- Give everyone a role—utilize each other's talents.

- Pick up some slack that you may not have been able to do while working.

- Make time for each other. Do things you both/all enjoy. Keep it simple and inexpensive—hike, bike, swim, picnic, barbecue, go to the library, or invite friends over for a game night.

- Do simple home projects that don't interfere with financial plans.

Ideas to Use with Social and Business Friends

- Put them at ease about talking to you about the job change and transition.

- Explain, generally, why you're looking for work, but don't let them lead you into a blame game or to trivialize the situation.

- Maintain control and direction of conversations and keep them positive.

- Ask for help in networking, such as leads, names, and introductions to people in their industry and personal network.

- Ask them to review your résumé.

- Stay connected, as long as possible, not just through your job search.

For those who don't have family nearby, close personal friends may be able to offer much of the support and encouragement we have discussed.

THIRD: TAKE CHARGE OF YOUR CHANGE— IMMEDIATELY

Don't wait another day. Yes, that means don't take the next couple of days, weeks or months off to "recuperate" from losing your job and to re-energize your internal battery. Don't fall into the rationalization that says, "I deserve a break considering how hard I've worked for all these years."

Lethargy is not the beginning of winning a new job. It opens the door to a pity party you may have been invited to, but believe me, you do not want to attend. The following four steps will set you in a better, more profitable and enjoyable direction:

1. Recognize each stage of emotion mentioned above for what it is and deny any counterproductive emotions to stall your progress to success. Set goals and determine success indicators (or milestones) that you can celebrate when you reach them. Give yourself a pat on the back.

2. Allow some opportunity to relish little successes, even if not directly involved with your job search, such as, having cleaned out the garage, closets or drawers, committing to an exercise routine, connecting with family and friends, creating some traditions that will survive the job search (family movie night at home, cards or game night, weekly visit to a volunteer organization, make a meaningful spiritual connection).

3. Create and invigorate your network, stay connected, don't withdraw, hibernate, or isolate yourself. (In person, on-line, by phone—all three!) Make everyone you know aware that you are taking a new step in your life and that they might be able to help!

4. Establish coping strategies, especially for anger. Anger saps energy. Get professional help, if you believe it will help. There is no shame in accessing an outside, helpful perspective.

FOURTH: ASSESS WHO YOU ARE AND WHAT YOU WANT TO BE

Explore all your options and opportunities. You may choose a new job, your own business, back to school, career switch, or a new industry. Your options are commensurate with your expectations. Don't belittle them. Open your thought to all possibilities, some you never dreamed of and some you may have dreamed of all of your life. Regardless of the economy, the unemployment rate, and other inhibiting news, the choice of what you want to do is still yours to make.

If It's a new Job you truly want, think about what you want to do and for what company. Consider what you do well and what you don't do well or don't want to do. Take into account what gives you a feeling of accomplishment. Also, think about what kind of boss you want and need. It's been shown time and again when people leave a job voluntarily, they don't leave companies—they leave bosses.

Assess your skills. Be honest with yourself. Will your current skill level carry you forward?

- How does your background, experience, and education compare to successful people in your desired new job?

- Do you need additional training in your profession?

- Do you need more education?

- Do you have the fundamental learning/skills development for a mid-career change?

It's not just about what makes you happy, it's also about what you are good at, the quality of your work, and the results you can achieve.

If you find a weakness, determine what actions you need to take to improve your value to a company. A vast majority of Hiring Managers will applaud these efforts and recognize you as the kind of problem-solver they're seeking.

Know what obstacles may stand in your way. They could trip you up and stop you from accomplishing the things you want. You want to avoid:

- Poor planning
- Procrastination
- Emotional distractions
- Distress
- A feeling of being overwhelmed or stressed out
- Low self-esteem
- Lack of confidence in your abilities
- Thinking you aren't worthy
- Comparing yourself unfavorably to others
- Accepting pressure (real or imagined) from your family or friends

These unhealthy emotions are self-defeating and only result in self-fulfilling prophecies. They are a waste of your time, drain your energy, throw cold water on your enthusiasm, and hold you in a state of mental paralysis.

When feeling overwhelmed, check to see if you are not attempting to accomplish too much at one time. Break the big overwhelming project into smaller, doable tasks. You'll find you can finish these smaller tasks and the overall project much more easily and quickly. And that bugaboo feeling of being overwhelmed will dissipate.

Break the big overwhelming project into smaller, doable tasks.

The great thing about thinking and emotions, good or bad, is that *you can control* them. You are not a puppet at the mercy of some emotional puppeteer.

Take, for instance, if you burn your hand due to placing it on a hot stove, you learn not to place your hand on a hot stove. The same goes for unhealthy emotions. If you feel overwhelmed, step back and take time to breathe. When you have these emotions under control, you will find that you can think of ways to overcome the challenges resulting from those emotions.

Summary

Personal preparation of thought, emotions and spirit is the solid foundation upon which you build a successful job search that culminates in winning the job you want.

- You can control negative thoughts and emotions through inner strength.

- Losing your previous job is not the end of the world. It is nothing more than a form of change. It's what you make of that change that makes all the difference in the world. Respond—don't react!

- Don't look back   and move forward.

- To successfully move forward to a new job, look where you're going, not just where you've been.

  o Don't constantly rehash what happened, who's to blame and why you don't have a job.

  o Ask for and encourage support from your family and friends.

  o Give everyone a role—utilize each other's talents.

  o Explain to others why you're looking for work, but don't let them lead you into a blame game or to trivialize the situation; maintain direction and control conversations to keep them positive.

- Ask for help in networking: leads, names and introductions to people in an industry you're interested in.

- Take charge of your change—immediately! Set goals and determine success indicators (or milestones) that you can celebrate when you reach them. Give yourself a pat on the back.

- Allow yourself time to relish small successes, both related and unrelated to your job search.

- Establish coping strategies.

- Assess who you are and who you want to be. Explore all your options—a new job, going into business for yourself.

- Assess your skills—do you need additional education and/or training?

- Consider what may be in your way—determine and build a defense against potential obstacles that would trip you up in your quest for a new job.

PREPARE YOURSELF FINANCIALLY FOR THE TRANSITION PERIOD

Earlier, we said that you already have a new job as the CEO of your own job search. As with any new business, you need to develop an educated estimate of how much this new venture will cost in time, effort, and money.

Time—estimate a best case, likely case, and worst-case scenario based on:

- What's going on in your industry and profession.

- What's happening with your regional economy, as well as, the national economy.

- What your geographic preferences are.

- What, if any, additional education or training you may need.

- How flexible you are regarding the job, salary, benefits, and geographic location you want.

Note: The time involved in doing a job search may be more in your control than you think it is. We discuss why this is true in Secret 3 on developing and using a job search marketing plan.

Effort—what it will take to achieve your goal of winning a new job based on:

- Your commitment to your job search—the amount of time you are willing and able to devote to it.

- Your desire to develop and use a marketing plan.

- Your willingness to build and use a job search network.

- Your comfort zone with "selling" yourself to Hiring Managers.

Money—how much your job search will cost based on:

- How you will finance it while maintaining an acceptable standard of living for you and your family.

Time and effort will be addressed in future secrets in this book. We will focus here on financing your job search without sacrificing your needs and those of your family. Please note that we said the "needs" of you and your family, not "wants." Unless you are totally flush with funds to last several months or more, you may have to pull back on some of those "wants." Let's take a look. The first step is to review your personal financial health to see:

- What the state of your finances are now.
- What monies you'll need for the near future.
- What you must do to ensure you have those funds.

YOUR PERSONAL FINANCIAL REVIEW

Remember what we said in part one of this secret: "Don't panic." We repeat that instruction here as well because this is where you need the courage of your conviction that you can find a new job—and do it without sacrificing everything. So, let's take this step-by-step.

FIRST: ANALYZE PRESENT INCOME SOURCES

Include, in this analysis, only that income (calculated on a monthly basis) that is relevant to you and your immediate family. Will you receive (or have you already received) income from your previous employer? Are you eligible to claim unemployment? Do you have any other business related income, such as, self-employment, a partnership, stocks, or close corporations?

SECOND: APPRAISE ASSETS

What other sources of income do you have: interest and dividends, commissions, social security, monthly pension payments, alimony? What about disability benefits or workman's compensation? Do you have any source of recurring income such as from an online business? Do you have access to low-interest, short-term loans?

Review your financial picture with the courage of your conviction that you can find a new job without sacrificing everything.

What cash do you have on hand and in the bank? What stocks and bonds and/or stock options or restricted stocks and brokerage accounts do you have? Does anyone owe you money? What's the cash value of any insurance you may have? Do you have equity in any real estate property? And finally, do you own any valuable collectables, art, jewelry, precious metals?

Also, include (only for tabulating your assets, not for drawing upon these) your IRAs, 401Ks, and annuities to provide you with a complete financial snapshot.

THIRD: EVALUATE PRESENT EXPENSES

As with income, include only those expenses that are relevant to you and your family. Examine where and then why you are spending money on each expense to provide you with a clear understanding on whether that expense is a need or a want. Review all your monthly expenses carefully and aggressively to see where you can reduce or eliminate them—temporarily or permanently, if appropriate.

Think ERMA, and Consider Whether You Can

- **E***liminate* an expense, such as that associated with using an ATM card; just walk into the bank and cash a check for free!

- **R***educe* an expense, such as buying a pair of $35 jeans instead of a pair that costs $135!

- **M***aintain* an expense, which must stay as is, such as your car payment (but check first!).

- **A***dd* an expense, such as the cost of a visit to the dentist to repair a broken tooth.

Some Possible Expenses

Let's review your expenses more closely. We've broken these down into nine categories:

- Home-related expenses
- Automotive and other Transportation expenses
- Insurance expenses
- Family-related expenses
- Children expenses
- Professional Services expenses
- Taxes and other Compulsory expenses
- Miscellaneous
- General Liability

When reviewing each expense associated with these categories, calculate those expenses on a monthly basis. Download a free budget spreadsheet template file we designed for you from www.TheCareerSuite.com/budgettemplate. Save it on your local computer and use it to formulate your budget. You'll find it easy to use and very helpful. We encourage you to use it.

Let's Take a Look at Each of These Categories and Their Associated Expenses

Expenses related to your home: mortgages (first and second), property taxes, home insurance, utilities (electric, telephones, water/sewage, garbage), fuel oil/natural gas, paid TV (cable, satellite), pool maintenance, pest control, termite bond, security monitoring, homeowners association fees, service contracts on appliances, maid service, off-site storage, second home expenses, miscellaneous. This would also include: home maintenance and repair, such as: pool, windows, roof, landscape maintenance and irrigation, painting, fertilization.

Automotive and other transportation expenses: the cost for each vehicle—leasing/financing and fuel/oil expenses, wash/wax, maintenance and repairs, licenses and insurance, tolls and parking and for alternative transportation expenses (bus, car pool, train, etc.).

Insurance related expenses: life, health, vision, dental, long term care, pet insurance and liability umbrella.

Family-related personal expenses: memberships, subscriptions, hair, cosmetics and toiletries, clothing, dry cleaning/laundry, gifts, groceries, dining out, entertainment, charitable contributions, vacations, pet expenses, sports/hobbies.

Expenses associated with your children: school and college tuition, private lessons/tutoring, college fund, day care/nursery/babysitting, school supplies, lunch money, camp/other summer activities, uniforms, allowances.

Expenses related to professional services: professional dues, property management, accountant, legal, tax preparation, financial advisor, safe deposit box and real estate fees.

Taxes and other compulsory expenses: federal, state, and local income tax, FICA or self-employment taxes, Medicare payments, required union dues, required retirement payments, court ordered child support actually paid and court ordered alimony actually paid.

Miscellaneous expenses: computer and technology-related expenses such as: software, hardware, maintenance, Internet services, online business services and products; donations.

And ninth, general liabilities: loans you owe, support to others (other than alimony and child support), credit card debt, other credit debt and judgments.

DEVELOP A FINANCIAL ACTION PLAN

Now, you are ready for post analysis action steps to keep you financially sound. If you have a family, you should include them in determining where cuts can be made before putting it into force. But remember, your children should not have the final decision. That is yours and your spouse's or life partner's decision.

Start, and commit to keeping, a daily log for the duration of your job search of what you and family members spend. Be totally honest with yourself and ask that family members do the same to determine what is a "need" and what is a "want." Look for any low-hanging fruit, such as, frequent lunches and or dinners out, designer coffees, unnecessary single purpose use of your car, etc.

With cooperation from you and family members, you'll be able to temporarily reduce or eliminate many expenses. You may even discover some expenses can be eliminated permanently, once you really take note of what you're actually spending your money on.

Don't just accept that expenses, which you think are unchangeable, are unchangeable. There are times that bills can be adjusted—at least temporarily, if you speak with the right people. This includes credit cards, monthly mortgage payments, some utilities and similar. Don't let pride or embarrassment stop you. Ask! Remember, the worst they can say is no and quite often, they will say yes. You have nothing to lose and peace of mind to gain.

If you are currently out of debt, do everything you can to stay that way. Do not use any credit cards, unless it is an *absolute emergency.*

Sir Winston Churchill once told his staff not to disturb him during a certain time each day unless it was absolutely necessary. A member of his staff wisely asked the old statesman what he considered to be an emergency. Churchill smiled and said, "The armed invasion of Britain and nothing less!" You would be wise to define an emergency for you and your family along the lines of Churchill's standard and cut out the use of credit cards entirely.

Some Additional Shopping Advice

- Stay away from non-essential purchases and impulse buying places (like the mall!).

- Plan meals, purchase house brands, buy less expensive cuts of meat, drink fewer soft drinks and alcoholic beverages to lower grocery costs.

- Shop for what you need, not what you want.

- Stay away from designer labels unless you're in a consignment shop.

- Save on prescriptions by using generic brands (where appropriate) and shop online pharmacies for best deals.

- Look for good deals, online and at sales.

- Review your insurance plans for your home and car to see if you can safely and wisely reduce costs, e.g. eliminate collision if your car is five+ years old, increase your deductibles on your car and home to what you think you can afford if you were to have a claim.

- Go a hundred percent mobile to reduce your phone costs and pay for only those mobile services you need.

- Have fun for free: attend free events, borrow and loan CDs, DVDs, books, etc.

- Consider bartering for products and services you need.

Summary

Developing and sticking to a budget is absolutely necessary for the duration of your job search. It is also where you need the courage of your conviction that you can find a new job—and do it without sacrificing everything before you can do it.

- **First, analyze where any income will be coming from right now**. Include, in this analysis, only that income (calculated on a monthly basis) that is relevant to you and your immediate family.

- **Second, appraise your assets.** Consider what you can and cannot draw upon during the duration of your job search.

- **Third, evaluate your expenses.** Think ERMA, and consider whether you can or must:

  o **E**liminate an expense
  o **R**educe an expense
  o **M**aintain an expense (Must stay as is)
  o **A**dd an expense

- **Fourth, develop a financial action plan**. You should include family members in determining where cuts can be made before putting it into force.

  o Start, and commit to keeping, a daily log for the duration of your job search of what you and family members spend.

  o Don't just accept that expenses you think are unchangeable are unchangeable. Many can be adjusted.

○ If you are currently out of debt, do everything you can to
stay that way. Do not use any credit cards unless an *abso-lute emergency.*

Secret 2:

SELL YOUR SIZZLE AND WIN
THE JOB YOU WANT

Success Story

An interviewer, who just offered Margo a job as accounts payable supervisor, surprised her with this statement, "For someone who doesn't appear to have any marketing in your background, you certainly put together a sales package geared to hiring you. And I definitely bought it!"

To say that Margo felt a glow inside when she heard this is a huge understatement. When she began learning how to develop a personal job search marketing plan, she thought it was far beyond her capabilities.

Like so many job seekers, her job search was comprised mainly of three parts. She wrote a résumé with cover letter and sent it to several companies that interested her. She even tried a little networking. When it came to an interview, well, it generally was hit or miss. Even the interviews where she thought she did well, did not conclude with her being hired.

As a result, like the other many job seekers, her job search was ineffective. And like them, she didn't know what else she should and could do. When Margo first heard that she needed to develop and use a personal job search marketing plan, she thought, "If that's what it takes to get a job in today's job market, I'm sunk. My background is finance, not marketing. Quite honestly, I'm not even sure I know what marketing really is!"

But she was intrigued, especially when she heard that a marketing plan would tie all her efforts together to make the greatest impact with a company's Hiring Manager. She immediately saw the value of that and eagerly said, "Okay, show me that I can do this."

That openness transformed her job search and showed Margo how to focus on and highlight what she had to offer a company. Her marketing plan enabled her to:

- Research companies and jobs that interested her and to incorporate this information in her overall plan and implementation.

- Develop her unique selling proposition and to position herself as a strong problem-solver in the eyes of Hiring Managers.

- Build and take advantage of a network of supporters who could introduce her to potential employers.

- Design and use targeted marketing materials such as résumés, cover letters, and follow-up materials to help reinforce her value to a company.

- Interview with confidence and a clear purpose in mind to prove her value to the Hiring Manager.

The synergy of these targeted, professional marketing tools gave her the strength, confidence and flexibility to succeed.

Remember: regardless of your business background, you will be able to follow the simple steps you can find in **"Sell Your Sizzle and Win the Job You Want."** *This is our online training/coaching program that takes you step by step through developing and implementing your targeted personal marketing plan. Visit www.TheCareerSuite.com for more information. You, like Margo, can put together a personal job search marketing plan like a pro!*

The Successful Marketing Plan

The information we gathered from interviews, with Hiring Managers, in various industries, throughout the country, led to a number of powerful conclusions that we turned into secrets. And the first conclusion we arrived at is pure gold for every savvy job seeker:

"To Succeed in Today's Job Search, Seekers Must Design and Use a Targeted Marketing Plan That They Effectively Execute to Win the Job They Want."

The true value of a marketing plan is that it helps the seller define the part of a market niche that he or she wants to target, and to focus his or her efforts solely on reaching and motivating the customers in that niche, to buy his or her product or services.

For the job seeker, that means a well thought-out marketing plan will enable you to build a clear picture of the industry that interests you. With it, you can develop a comprehensive profile of the companies you want to target as potential employers.

It will allow you to devote all your time, effort and finances on what will bring you the fastest and best results—meeting the needs and wants of those companies.

Each step you take to implement your marketing plan will build on the previous one. In this way, you concentrate the strength of who you are, what you've done, and where you've been in your career to sell yourself in the best light possible, so that a Hiring Manager makes his decision in your favor. The result is a more effective job search and winning the job you want more quickly and with less stress.

Great News! You Don't Need an MBA

Don't let the idea of developing and using a marketing plan throw you off or discourage you. You may be thinking, "Are you kidding? I don't know anything about marketing. There is no way I can do this." But, you don't need an MBA (Master of Business Administration) to do this!

These secrets work whether you are applying to be the vice president of operations, the manager of information systems, an administrative assistant, a waiter, a plant foreman, an engineer, a drafting assistant, a writer, a warehouse operator, or the president. The secrets are universal and can work for any job search! And they are easy to follow, too.

You may think that marketing plans are some mysterious business tool that only MBAs or marketing gurus understand and can use. That's simply not true. They're really common sense guidelines that tie all the various elements of a successful job search together to make your job search:

1. Smarter, to give you an unbeatable competitive edge to sell yourself.

2. More flexible, to enable you to quickly change parts to be as effective as possible.

3. Stronger, to provide you with the proof a Hiring Manager needs to choose you over all other competing job seekers.

4. More organized and effective, to help keep you on the right path toward your ultimate goal of getting a job more quickly and with less stress.

What you need is desire, a willingness to learn, and maybe to get out of your comfort zone, especially if you got nervous at the mention of that four letter word "sell" in relation to "yourself."

Job Seekers: If you think you can or if you think you can't, you're right!

Don't say you don't have the confidence, because *everyone* has confidence. Remember; either you're confident you *can* do something or you're confident you *can't*, but you are definitely confident! It's up to you to make the best choice.

Use a targeted plan of approach to your job search and you will build a solid foundation of confidence to do what you need to do to get the job you want—quickly and with no wasted effort.

"The Whole Is Greater Than the Sum of Its Parts"

You've probably heard that saying many times before, especially if you've ever been on a team—in sports or business. A job search marketing plan helps you build and sharpen the parts of your job search like members of a team—your research, résumé and cover letter, networking opportunities, interviews, follow-up, and job offer negotiation.

When you develop those job search members—or parts and order them through a well thought-out job search marketing plan, the combined effect makes a much stronger impact toward successfully getting you the job you want. And there really are only five basic steps to developing an effective marketing plan that enables you to hit the bull's eye of a new job.

THE FIVE BASIC STEPS TO YOUR SUCCESSFUL JOB SEARCH MARKETING PLAN

Step One: Get the inside scoop on any company you're interested in.

Step Two: Find out what's important to a Hiring Manager and make it just as important to you.

Step Three: Become a "hero" to the Hiring Manager—then make him a hero to his company.

Step Four: Stay uppermost in the Hiring Manager's mind to get the job you want—now.

Step Five: Super-size your sales skills and remember to ask for the sale—your job.

Let's take these steps one-at-a-time to build your confidence in the ability to accomplish this task and make your task of seeking a job easier and quicker to achieve.

Just like a marketing plan for a major national product, your job search marketing plan is built on a solid foundation of research.

STEP ONE: GET THE INSIDE SCOOP ON COMPANIES YOU'RE INTERESTED IN

The first step of building any marketing plan is to get to know the customer. Successful sales people can't say enough about how important knowing a customer is. Corporate marketing departments spend large amounts of time, effort, and money trying to understand what and why their customers buy what they buy. You don't need to spend a lot of money, but you do need to spend some time and effort on learning about your "customers"—the companies that appeal to you and their Hiring Managers.

How do you do this? Research. Research. Research. Don't worry—there are tons of resources at your finger-tips online and offline, many of which are free, that can easily provide you with as much information as you're willing to discover about companies you target in your job search campaign. Here are a few you will want to keep in mind:

- Your networking contacts
- DunandBradstreet.com
- Hoovers.com
- Corporateinformation.com
- Google.com
- Yahoo.com

And be sure to visit the website of each company that interests you for information about the inner workings of the organization: its values, products, and vision.

Now that you know someplace to begin your research, what do you want to find out? You need to arm yourself with vital information about companies you're interested in. That means, for example, finding out:

- The company's immediate business needs.
- The company's future direction, vision, or goals.
- What opportunities and challenges may factor into that company's success.

Once you start digging, you'll find other important pieces of information that will give you a clear picture of what a company's all about. Have at it. The more you know about that company, the more prepared you'll be to stand out from other job seekers with a targeted response to their needs.

You'll find this kind of information will help you get your foot in the door and help you shine when in front of Hiring Managers. It shows him or her that you have done your homework. It will demonstrate that you care about the company, as well as, yourself.

Then, you'll be able to effectively address the seven "P"s of marketing and selling:

1. **Product** (you)

2. **Packaging** (how you will present yourself to potential employers)

3. **People** (your networking channels for referrals)

4. **Promotion** (your story—talents, experience, accomplishments—and how it relates to your customer's needs and wants)

5. **Physical environment** (your competition in the job market)

6. **Process** (your strategy and tactics designed and used to reach your goal—winning the job you want)

7. **Price** (your salary requirements and points of negotiation)

Each of the elements of your job search—your research, résumé and cover letter, networking opportunities, interviews, follow-up, and job offer negotiation is influenced by the seven "P"s and vice versa. Now, don't go crazy saying, "I can't think of all this." You already do. You just may not be aware of it.

Think of the last job you had. How were you dressed when you interviewed, what did you talk about, and what did you include in your negotiation when offered the job? Your answers showed you already considered your product, packaging, promotion, and process when it came to research, an interview, negotiation, and probably a number of other elements in your job search. You may not have been aware you were doing this, or why some of the things you did worked and why some didn't.

If that is the case, you may have been what is called an "unconscious competent." You did the right things, but didn't know why they were right. In your job search, you want to be a "conscious competent." You want to do the right things and know why and how they're right. Then you can easily replicate what works and quickly change what doesn't. Working your job search marketing plan helps you achieve conscious competency status.

And being a "conscious competent" enables you to better position yourself, so a Hiring Manager *sees the benefits in hiring you* instead of another job seeker. Do your homework before meeting a Hiring Manager and you can more effectively tie your talents, knowledge, experience and accomplishments to the needs of his company. In this way, you'll be the job seeker who truly demonstrates a sincere interest in and concern for the company, as well as yourself. You'll be the job seeker who demonstrates why you're *uniquely qualified* to fill the open job. And it all begins with researching and understanding your customer—your potential employer.

STEP TWO: FIND OUT WHAT'S IMPORTANT TO A HIRING MANAGER—MAKE IT IMPORTANT TO YOU

You also want to learn as much as you can about any Hiring Manager you may speak with during the hiring process. This enables you to see the hiring process and the company's needs from his perspective. Since he is doing the hiring, there's no better perspective to use!

You see, thinking like a Hiring Manager helps you outshine all other job seekers. And it's a vital step in developing your winning marketing plan, one that puts your job search in overdrive to obtain the job you want. It allows you to get "inside his head" and to think like he does about what kind of person will best meet his company's needs.

Put Yourself in the Hiring Manager's Shoes for a Minute

Imagine you're the Hiring Manager interviewing a job applicant who shows that he knows your company's needs and understands your needs in the hiring process. The applicant also easily and naturally relates everything he tells you about himself to those needs. In essence, he's built his "sales pitch" from your perspective.

That's impressive by any standard and helps you see why he stands out from the crowd of other job seekers.

In your job search, when you see things from the perspective of the Hiring Manager—when you get inside his head—you then understand and appreciate his needs and those of his company. Just as a successful sales person recognizes and uses such information about his customer to make a sale, you, as the job seeker, must do the same with your customer—the Hiring Manager and his company.

We can't emphasize this enough. Thinking like the Hiring Manager, especially in an interview, empowers you like nothing else. That's because you speak the Hiring Manager's language.

You prove your understanding of his needs by showing him how your talents, knowledge, experience, and accomplishments can benefit his company. You continually and effectively link your "brand" to his brand to build the "customer loyalty" that will naturally lead him to decide to hire you.

This takes a little more digging than the research you do about a company. However, it can be done. Remember, your next job may depend on it, so the effort to gather this kind of information will be well spent. Some resources to use here will include your networking contacts.

First-hand knowledge about a Hiring Manager is invaluable. You can also Google him. Here you may be able to find what organizations he belongs to, what awards he's received and articles he may have authored. All of these types of demographic information will provide insight into what makes him "tick." And that provides the insight on how to position and promote yourself to this very important customer.

"You" Are Your Brand

Then, take the understanding you gathered from your research of a company and respective Hiring Managers. Blend it with what you know about yourself. Use your job search marketing plan to develop the strategy and tactics needed to help you develop and sell your "brand," you.

Remember, being unemployed doesn't mean you are out of work. On the contrary, you're performing the most important work you can ever perform. You're seeking your next job. You're the CEO of your own job search. It's *your* responsibility to sell yourself. And that includes developing a "brand" for your product—*you*—that is memorable; one that leaves a positive impression on the Hiring Manager.

Use your marketing plan to develop the strategy and tactics to develop and sell your "brand."

A brand, with regards to your job search, is an image, thought or concept you want Hiring Managers to have of you that positively positions you in a Hiring Manager's mind. It's your responsibility to develop and establish this brand; to present yourself in such a way that every time the Hiring Manager thinks about you, he immediately relates it to the image you want him to have.

This is where the marketing plan process shines. It forces you to think through who and what you are in relation to your business life. By defining and expanding this "revelation" about yourself, you can develop a unique identity on which to build your brand. To help you establish a brand that stands out, answer these two questions:

1. What image do you want the Hiring Manager to have about you as a job seeker? What qualities do you want him to associate with you?

2. How can you most effectively position and promote yourself so this is the image Hiring Managers immediately think of—the image of the job seeker of choice?

When you begin to think like a Hiring Manager, when you understand and appreciate his and his company's needs, then you'll have the answers and can take the actions that will produce a memorable positive brand.

STEP THREE: BECOME A "HERO" TO A HIRING MANAGER—THEN MAKE HIM A HERO TO HIS COMPANY

So far, in your marketing plan, you've gathered vital information about companies that interest you. You've gained insight into how and why Hiring Managers think what they do about their company's need. You've developed a brand for yourself that speaks to these needs in a specifically meaningful way.

The next step is to prove *you're* the hero of this story. Consider this hero's story:

Samir is an advertising director at a large consumer foods company. One of his main responsibilities is leading the creative concept and production of commercials for legacy products—the products that built the reputation for his company—but aren't as popular as they once were with today's shoppers.

The only job seeker who extracts Excalibur is the job seeker who is a highly skilled problem-solver – the "hero" of his story.

Last week, he came out of Jeff's office (his boss, the EVP of marketing) and was barely able to contain his excitement! Jeff had just told Samir that the commercial he produced for (product name withheld) gave the Legacy Products Division a twelve percent increase over plan for the quarter. It also pulled the product back from the brink of extinction.

Jeff asked Samir, "How does it feel to be a star? What you just accomplished is nothing short of a minor miracle and is making us both look golden. The stock took a jump today on the news and we're all going to get fatter bonuses because of your good work. Needless to say, I am proud of you and more than pleased with the contribution you make to this team and the company."

Samir was on cloud nine! He knew that tired, old brand still had a lot of life left in it. No one else seemed to have the same confidence. His new ad approach proved it, however. He was now even more confident that his hard work and perseverance was worth all the effort.

Needless to say, this was a really big win for Samir and for his boss, Jeff. He was a hero to his boss and, in turn, they both looked like heroes to the company. A giant win for them both!

The next time Samir is in front of a Hiring Manager, this is exactly the kind of story he needs to relate. It is strong evidence that he has what it takes to make a significant contribution to a company. A savvy Hiring Manager is going to want that kind of heroics on his team.

You now need to prove to the Hiring Manager you are the only one who can pull Excalibur (you know, the sword!) out of the stone in which it was thrust. This is where you need to refine the strategy and tactics of your marketing plan. Everything you do and say about yourself, all the facts and figures you share with a Hiring Manager must strengthen this picture and establish you as the hero.

You need to focus the strategy and tactics of your marketing plan on your experience, talent and accomplishments *as they relate to the company's goals and objectives*. This is vital. Everything about you must be real, truthful and authentic.

Marketing is not fluff. When done correctly, it's positioning the truth in the most convincing way.

If you consistently relate the facts about what you bring to the table for his company, you show the Hiring Manager you are able to solve problems, meet needs and help his company achieve its goals. Demonstrate how you can be the problem-solver for him—and you become the hero he's seeking. This is why being truthful about your experience and accomplishments is absolutely imperative.

Another reason the truth is vital is that being a true problem-solving hero puts a halo on your head. And, in the eyes of your new colleagues, the "brilliant" Hiring Manager, who was able to recruit such a talented person, shares that halo. He becomes a hero in their eyes, as well. But, if you oversold yourself or don't deliver what you promised on the job, there is nothing worse for a Hiring Manager than to have to reverse that hiring decision because your promises were empty.

STEP FOUR: MOVE TO AND STAY "UPPERMOST IN MIND" TO GET THE JOB YOU WANT—NOW

The final step in your marketing plan is to make sure everything you do and say for yourself in your job search embodies AIDA (acronym for Attention, Interest, Desire, and Action) to put you and keep you number one in the mind of the Hiring Manager. This marketing tool has been around since the birth of advertising and still holds true, especially in today's tight job market. Every aspect of your marketing plan has to contain each and all of these elements to achieve the goal you want—to establish you as the top candidate of the Hiring Manager's list.

What exactly is AIDA and what does it mean? AIDA is a time-tested, easy-to-use and effective way to get greater response from a marketing strategy, especially in your job search campaign. It means:

A: **Attention**—*attract it.*
I: **Interest**—*hold it.*
D: **Desire**—*build it.*
A: **Action**—*encourage it.*

The AIDA model is fairly simple and continues to be the most effective conceptual model for creating targeted marketing communication messages. And remember, everything you say, write and do is a marketing message that reinforces your brand—and your potential for getting the job you want. The goal you achieve, by incorporating AIDA into your job search marketing plan and materials, is to build value and excitement in the Hiring Manager's mind. And you do that by identifying benefits, benefits and more benefits—all related to the Hiring Manager's needs.

Attention: Regardless of the marketing tool, if your brand doesn't immediately get the attention of the Hiring Manager, you've lost him for good. You must gain his attention to have an opportunity to deliver your message. Whether you're developing a networking letter, targeted résumé, interviewing strategy or other job search marketing tool, get the Hiring Manager's attention by:

- Citing a relevant statistic or fact about yourself (your brand) that ties in with the Hiring Manager's and company's needs or goals.

- Make a declarative statement about how you benefitted a previous employer and how that experience can benefit the company that interests you.

- Ask questions to show both your understanding of a company's needs and your interest in helping them reach their goals.

- Make an offer to follow-up an interview with information of value to the Hiring Manager.

- Use a testimonial from a previous employer or colleague that shows what you've done in the past is a strong indication that you'll be an asset to the company that interests you.

Keep this aspect simple and on point and you'll be more assured of success.

Here is an example of citing a relevant statistic or fact about yourself:

> "I have a reputation for taking a fading brand, as I did with Chanel N^O 5, and breathing fresh life into it. It's back to number one in global fragrance sales."

- Did you initiate a process that significantly decreased a company's overhead?

- Did you make a sale that significantly increased a company's revenue?

- Did you overcome substantial obstacles to complete an assigned project on time and under budget?

Consider including that success in your marketing tools. It is sure to gain the Hiring Manager's attention because you're speaking his language and to his need!

Interest: After you've gained the Hiring Manager's attention, follow up with enough information to encourage him to continue reading and listening. Persuade him by showing what you can do for him based on what you've done for others. Build his interest and trigger the emotions that will make him feel good about interviewing/hiring you.

> "In 2011, I provided all Integra sales managers with full understanding of the mechanics behind the new product line, which resulted in a successful launch within one week and one hundred percent market share by getting there fast and first. I know I can do the same for your innovative Biotread product as well."

Desire: Deep inside every Hiring Manager there are two desires—the desire to succeed by hiring the best person to fit the job in his organization—and the desire to avoid the failure of either not finding an acceptable candidate, or worse, hiring the wrong person.

> "My track record speaks for itself. When working with a new author, I have never missed a deadline or failed to meet an agreed upon goal. Your new authors will get the same kind of support from me."

All your marketing materials (résumés, cover letters, follow-up materials) or your face-to-face meetings should speak to his desire to succeed and be a "hero" to everyone who will work with you. It should speak to his desire to avoid the pain of the mistake in hiring the wrong person.

Some ways to generate desire are to:

- Lower the Hiring Manager's risk in meeting with you and offering you the job.

- Demonstrate your credibility.

- Offer a testimonial or case study of results you've achieved.

- Show how you may help them.

Action: The call to action (in job search marketing materials) is you asking for an interview, for a job, or for the compensation package you want. This is your call to action and in it, you give the Hiring Manager enough motivation for him to take the action that fulfills his needs and the purpose of your marketing plan—to win the job you want—*now*.

> "I'd really like to have the opportunity to put my proven methods of converting audience members into lifetime donors to work for you and the Sada Tremont Performing Arts Center."

STEP FIVE: SUPER-SIZE YOUR SALES SKILLS AND REMEMBER TO ASK FOR THE SALE—THE JOB

The final step is to implement your marketing plan. And that takes a super sales person—*you*. After all, no one has a more vested interest in your success than you do. So, no one can do a better sales job than you—when you know how.

Most successful salesmen follow a simple five step sales process. You should learn this process and follow it religiously. It will produce the results you want!

First—establish rapport with customers. This builds credibility and trust. Does he have a picture of his children on his desk? Talk about that. Do you see awards on the wall? Find one you can relate to and talk about that. People want to do business with people they trust.

Second—discover the problems and the opportunities of your customers. Ask the Hiring Manager questions to uncover the difficulty and also the success the company is experiencing.

Third—champion the best solution. Show the Hiring Manager, based on what you know about the company, how your experience and talents can help solve his problems and take advantage of potential opportunities.

Fourth—support the Hiring Manager's individual needs related to the company's needs. Empathize with his needs, desires, and challenges. Demonstrate how hiring you will make him a "hero" in his company. In other words, show him the benefits of hiring you.

Fifth, and finally—close the sale. Use trial closes throughout the interview: gain the Hiring Manager's agreement to points you make through each step in the sales process.

Some examples might be:

> "Sounds like the direction you plan to take with your general ledger conversion is almost exactly what I was able to accomplish in my last job with their PQR general ledger conversion. Is that correct?"

> "Is PQR general ledger experience something you are specifically looking for in a department manager?"

> "I have successfully trained over two hundred accountants in the use of the PQR general ledger. Would training experience be valuable to you in the conversion process?"

Attain small agreements, like these, as you proceed through your interview. When you reach the final close—whether it's asking for the job outright or seeking an additional meeting or just an indication of his interest in hiring you—he will recognize that you have eliminated any reason to say no at that point.

Don't be afraid to ask for the job—if it seems appropriate. Use a final close—show your enthusiasm and ask for the job, if you really want it. This isn't begging, it's connecting skills and accomplishments with needs and opportunities and coming to a logical decision to hire!

For example:

> Craig has been through three rounds of interviews with Judy, the new VP of Finance for Broadway Productions. He is one of two final candidates and is confident his organizational, financial, and diplomatic skills are a great fit for the job.

Judy needs someone seasoned and not afraid to work with investors, producers, directors and stage talent. Her job is to keep the funding flowing and to keep scrupulous account of finances for the investors. Craig is a master at all of this.

He could really identify with actors auditioning for a part. He knew he had the talent. His past experience with Nightlife Theatrical was a perfect fit. He also had a love for the theater, and frankly, really liked Judy and wanted to see her succeed in her new job. He felt like saying, "Pick me, pick me!," but knew that would seal his fate—and not in a good way.

Instead, he relied on his confidence and track record and said, "We have had the opportunity to get to know each other a bit, and I think your need for a strong administrative and financial partner and my skills and experience supporting multiple senior executives at Nightlife Theatrical look like a perfect match. I'd love to have the opportunity to prove what I can do to help you get your systems and relationships grounded and operating at peak performance to impress the heck out of Broadway Productions."

The number one conclusion we arrived at from all our interviews with Hiring Managers is to think like them—gather industry and company information; build your memorable brand; develop a personal marketing plan; and be the successful sales person who wins you the job you want. Thinking like a Hiring Manager puts you on the right path and helps you focus everything you do and say on achieving your *primary* objective—to get the job you want—quickly. So, begin the right way, right now.

Summary

Know you're already employed as the CEO of your own job search firm. It's *your* responsibility to *sell* yourself. And that includes developing a marketing plan to serve as your road map to a new job.

As the CEO of your own job search firm, you must build a "brand" for your product—*you*—that is memorable; one that leaves a positive impression on the Hiring Manager. You do this with the help of a well-thought-out marketing plan.

The true value of a job search marketing plan is that it helps you:

- Define that part of a market (a niche) and the companies therein that you want to target.

- Focus your efforts solely on reaching and motivating the companies and Hiring Managers in that niche to make you their candidate of choice.

- Build a clear picture of the industry you're interested in.

- Devote all your time, effort and finances on what will bring you the fastest and best results—meeting the needs and wants of those companies.

It doesn't take an MBA in marketing to develop and use an effective marketing plan.

> It takes desire, the willingness to learn, belief in yourself and the confidence to reflect the best of who and what you are to sell yourself to a company and its Hiring Manager.

There are five basic steps to developing and using a job search marketing plan:

1. Get the inside scoop on any company you're interested in.

- The first step of building any marketing plan is to get to know the customer. This takes research—on the Internet, in annual reports, etc.

- This kind of information will help you get your foot in the door and help you shine before Hiring Managers.

Do your homework before meeting a Hiring Manager and you can more effectively tie your talents, knowledge, experience and accomplishments to the needs of his company. In this way, you'll be the ideal job applicant, who truly demonstrates a sincere interest in and concern for the company as well as yourself and who demonstrates why you're uniquely qualified to fill the open job.

2. Find out what's important to a Hiring Manager and make it just as important to you. Think like a Hiring Manager to outshine all other job seekers; getting "inside his head" helps you think as he does about what he needs to meet his company's needs.

   Focus the strategy and tactics of your marketing plan on your experience, talent and accomplishments as they relate to the company's and Hiring Manager's goals and objectives and build a memorable "brand" that inspires customer loyalty.

3. Become a "hero" to the Hiring Manager, then make him a hero to his company.

   - Consistently relate the facts about what you bring to the table to solve the Hiring Manager's needs and help the company achieve its goals.

   - Show how you can be the problem-solver for him and you become the hero he's seeking.

When done correctly, marketing is positioning the truth in the most convincing way. This is how you become the hero (or heroine) of your job search.

Stay foremost in the Hiring Manager's mind to get the job you want—now. Make sure everything you do and say in your job search embodies AIDA:

> Get **Attention**
> Hold **Interest**
> Arouse **Desire**
> Gain **Action**

The goal you achieve by incorporating AIDA into your marketing plan and marketing materials is to build value and excitement in the Hiring Manager's mind.

4. Super-size your Sales Skills and remember to ask for the sale—your job. Implement your marketing plan. And that takes a super sales person—*you*. No one has a more vested interest in your success than you do; and no one can do a better sales job when you know how.

Learn every successful salesman's five step sales process to ensure your success:

First—establish rapport with customers.

Second—discover the problems and the opportunities of your customers.

Third—champion the best solution.

Fourth—support the Hiring Manager's individual needs related to the company's needs.

Fifth—close the sale. Use trial closes and a final close.

RÉSUMÉS THAT OPEN THE DOOR TO JOB INTERVIEWS

Success Story

Jim was a forty-five-year-old retired army colonel with years of leadership experience. He had gone into the army right after college graduation and spent his entire career moving up through the ranks. His private industry experience was limited to one year, in restaurant management, immediately after retirement from the army.

When he took a close look at what he really wanted to do, he knew it was in training others in the restaurant business.

His first step was to research companies he was interested in. He scoured advertised job openings for a training manager and sent out several targeted résumés and cover letters and customized each one to speak directly to the needs of each restaurant company and each job description.

In all of them, he highlighted his extensive background in training new officers, managing people and grass roots capability in running restaurants—all core capabilities these companies needed.

What was the most interesting, in speaking with the manager that hired him, was hearing the Hiring Manager's first reaction. He thought, "No way can a guy at this point in his career step into a relatively new business situation and train others to be successful in it. But, his résumé got my attention. I would skeptically put it down and then pick it up again. I just couldn't let it go. Finally, I invited him in for an interview and the rest is history. He definitely was the right candidate and did a tremendous job in training many others to help them attain success in their careers, also."

Now that's what we call a résumé that sings! Jim didn't write his résumé from his perspective—what he wanted in a job—but the Hiring Manager's perspective—what the company and the Hiring Manager needed from a job candidate. You can do this as well, with the same results!

How To Gain a Face-To-Face Meeting

Basically, there really are only two effective ways for a job seeker to contact a Hiring Manager and gain a face-to-face interview:

1. Provide him with a dynamite résumé and cover letter that speaks directly to the job requirements and the needs of the organization and makes the Hiring Manager stop and take notice.

2. Attain a referral to the Hiring Manager from a trusted acquaintance—yours and his.

This secret discusses the purpose, value and strategies to incorporate into your résumés. (We'll discuss networking further in our next secret.)

And yes, we said résumés in the plural. The first and most important point in this secret for you to understand and take to heart is the need for *customizing* your résumés. Here is where you use the information you gathered in your earlier research from Secret 1 to fit your résumé to the profile (needs, goals, objectives and/or challenges) of each company you are interested in.

THE PURPOSE OF YOUR RÉSUMÉ

Numerous studies have shown that most job seekers know they need a résumé, but aren't clear why, other than it is customary to have one or it's just expected. Question: if you don't know the purpose of something, in this case a résumé, how can you effectively prepare one that will accomplish anything? So, to clarify the issue, the purpose of a job résumé is to accomplish two main objectives:

1. Represent you in the best light when you can't do so in person.

2. Create enough interest in the mind of the Hiring Manager (or the person who reviews résumés for them) so that they offer you:

- An exploratory interview.
- An interview for a specific job opening.

The most effective résumés create a picture in the mind of the Hiring Manager that shows them how you: (your background, accomplishments, education, results and so on)

- Can solve problems for them and their company.
- Can fit in with their team to accomplish great results

That's why you need more than one résumé. As in Jim's case, your résumé needs to speak *specifically* to each Hiring Manager: What his or her specific needs are for the job they are trying to fill now, what his or her needs may be in the future.

Remember: Your résumés need to provide critical information about you; it should "sell" you to the Hiring Manager and show:

- How you can fulfill the needs he has.
- How you fit with their team and company.
- That you can get things done.
- That you've had a positive impact with former employers.

Don't include anything negative in your résumé that might cause you to be passed over. You'll have an opportunity to address and resolve, in a positive way, any negatives in your background in an interview. Putting a negative in a résumé will get you screened *out* with no opportunity for an interview!

Insight from Hiring Managers on Résumés and Cover Letters

Are you ready to hear what the Hiring Managers told us about résumés and cover letters? Here are a few of the comments we received from them:

"Basics include a well-crafted résumé/letter that is succinct, free of errors and enables me to easily extract what he/she did, when and for whom. I don't like generalities or lots of narrative. Most successful, however, is a personal introduction by someone known to both of us."

"It is crucial to make sure that you meet the published requirements for the job [in the résumé]. Sometimes, you can be clever in restating your experience/qualifications, but you must be honest about the potential match, and let it go if there's simply no fit. Also, you must be honest with yourself about what your strengths are. Ex: If the job involves a lot of writing, and you are not particularly good at it (or it is laborious for you), look elsewhere!"

"Sending a résumé is often not enough in today's market—many of us HR leaders get a lot of résumés. A personal follow up call, or email, to inquire about the status of a résumé (frankly) forces us to address that particular request."

"For professional positions, the cover letter is key. Because every job I have requires good communication and writing skills, I always ask for a two to three page cover letter outlining aptitude and interest in the position. The best letters take the job description and, point by point, provide the detail of demonstrated success that tie to the job description. This kind of cover letter gives me a sample of the person's communication and writing skills. (The cover letter requirement also weeds out applicants and leaves me with fewer, but stronger applications—people that take the time to do this are serious about the job).

"Résumés do not get you selected—they get you screened out—so make your résumé with a very high level of quality, focus on the problems or challenges you saw or were given and how you solved them and the benefits your solutions created for the organization."

"A résumé free of errors, succinct and one that enables me to easily extract their potential value to my organization. Applicants tend to *look at what they can get rather than show what they can offer; and their résumés generally reflect that. That's too bad."*

"It must be professional, engaging, interesting. The best cover letter should outline a job seeker's aptitude and interest in the position."

"The best letters take the job description and provide the details of demonstrated success that tie to the job description."

The most insightful comment we heard from respondent Hiring Managers about résumés was: "If you don't put forth the effort to make your résumé look as good as possible, why would a Hiring Manager expect you to put forth the effort to do your best on the job?"

That comment is on target! Never forget it.

Savvy job seekers know their résumé and cover letter must speak directly to the Hiring Manager's needs and those of his company to get the interview.

From the Hiring Manger's Perspective

Put yourself in the Hiring Manager's chair. It will make a huge difference in how you approach and prepare your résumés and cover letters. We use the plural of these terms because it's vital that you *customize parts of your résumés.*

That means you should write a number of customized résumés and letters tailored to demonstrate your interest in specific companies. Every company is different, so broadcast mailings of a single résumé is just about useless, especially in today's tight job market.

Your résumé cannot be generic, and bland cover letters are pointless. Everything in a résumé and cover letter should be directed toward one goal: getting a specific interview at a particular company.

Your job experience, education, background, career objectives and summary statements should be uniquely targeted to an audience "of one" in a specific company and industry. Anything less reduces the likelihood you'll receive a request for an interview from the

Hiring Managers look for a concise and honest résumé.

Hiring Manager. Your résumé may never even reach a hiring authority, but will probably reach a trashcan, if not customized.

Keep in mind and don't miss the following when composing your résumé or your résumé may end up in the trash:

- Be accurate—don't lie or exaggerate! Companies check your references, degrees, etc.

- Focus on the past ten to fifteen years; longer than that can be listed, but not elaborated on—unless it is highly unique and was a springboard to your last ten to fifteen years.

- Keep it one to two pages in length—more than that is too long.

- The most important information goes on the top half of the first page.

- Write in the third person (no I, my, etc.).

- Avoid redundancy; don't repeat the same thing more than once in a résumé.

- Use positive and powerful language (avoid using words such as "helped," "assisted," and other words that indicate someone else was doing the "real" work and you were just there).

- Create clarity, consistency, and continuity.

Just as job networking is similar to an ad in which a trusted spokesperson talks about a product, your résumés and cover letters are the headline, subhead, body copy and call-to-action of that ad. In that ad, the copywriter writes with a specific audience "of one" in mind. He will use different attention-getting devices in each ad to perfectly target each specific audience.

Two Most Common Résumé Formats

The two most common formats for résumés are the *chronological* and *functional*. The chronological format is classic and most preferred by Hiring Managers and most often used by job seekers. It presents your background and experience in reverse chronological order starting with your most recent job first and proceeding backwards to your first. Each section is a complete description of each job.

The chronological résumé is particularly effective when:

- Your career has been in one general profession and or industry
- Your career shows progression of responsibility
- You have worked for premiere employers (IBM, General Electric, etc.)

Sample of a Chronological Résumé

Name

City, State   **E-mail address**   **Phone**

SUMMARY

Senior Financial Manager with strategic orientation and ability to develop and implement long-range business strategies. Proven track record of adding value to growing organizations through improved systems, operational efficiencies and acquisitions. Considered a quick learner, creative problem solver, team player and effective negotiator.

EXPERIENCE

Anderson Industries, Ford, Ohio   **2003—Present**
Third largest residential real estate broker in the US with over 2500 sales agents in 75 offices. Annual revenues approximately $285 million.

Senior Vice President / Chief Financial Officer
Responsible for all department operations of finance, acquisitions, accounting, information systems and facilities for Goody Realty and Equity Title Company. Managed staff of 30.

Accomplishments:

- Established strategic partnership to deliver graphic real estate information to agent users. This significant business relationship is the first ever between a real estate company and major information provider.

- Developed and implemented a new breakthrough commission plan, which met corporate, margin goals and agent requirements for upside incentive.

- Achieved over $5.2 million in internal and external expense reductions through contract renegotiations, automation and departmental restructuring. Absorbed a 20% volume increase with no additional headcount.

- Evaluated multiple business combination opportunities and completed the acquisition and integration of eight regional real estate brokers.

- Prepared road show presentation, investor relations strategy and SEC reporting format for the tax-free spin-off of Chicago Title from Zarbo Financial Corporation.

Bellco Corporation, Torrance City, Ohio   **1996—2003**

Chief Financial Officer / Secretary and Treasurer
Responsible for all areas of finance and administration including corporate planning and analysis, budgeting, shareholder relations and SEC reporting.

Accomplishments:

- Completed $19 million secondary and $6 million initial public offerings.

- Raised $19 million in private equity capital.

- Negotiated $11 million revolving bank credit line.

- Negotiated and completed two strategic acquisitions comprising more than $10 million in additional annual domestic and international revenue.

- Served as General Manager of catalog from 1987 until 1990. Catalog revenue increased from $800,000 to $3.2 million during this time.

- Managed several upgrades of corporate management information systems.

- Directly responsible for introduction of four significant new products.

Topps Computer Corporation, Boise, Idaho   **1993—1996**

Controller
Responsible for internal/external financial reporting, cash management, taxes, budgeting, financial analysis, and external financial relationships.

Accomplishments:
- Prepared financial and operating portion of company business plans, which were successful in raising over $24 million in private and venture capital financing.
- Managed selection and installation of ASK financial, cost, and MRP II management information system along with appropriate accounting and system controls.
- Designed and implemented company budget/forecast system completely integrated with the automated general ledger.

KPMG, Boise, Idaho   **1990—1993**

Senior Consultant
Responsible for planning, budgeting and performance of audit fieldwork and financial reporting including supervision, review and training of staff accountants, financial statement analysis, statistical modeling including linear regression and development of client relations. Received 1982 National Innovations Award for new client product.

EDUCATION
- University of Montana, Billings, Montana, Wilber, MBA, focus on Finance and Accounting
- University of Wyoming, Cheyenne, Wyoming, BA, Major in Finance, Minor in Economics

AFFILIATIONS
- Board of Directors, Regional Multiple Listing Service of Ohio
- American Institute of Certified Public Accountants
- MI Association of Realtors
- American Audubon Society

The second most common résumé format is the *functional résumé*. This kind of résumé typically focuses more on your competencies and skills and focuses less on the progression of your career and past employers.

Although functional résumés are used less frequently, they are particularly useful when:

- You have a significant time gap in employment.
- You have been out of the job market for a period of time.
- You want to focus on skills not used in most recent jobs.
- You have had a significant change in your profession or are seeking to make a significant change in your current job search.
- You have changed employers frequently.

Now let's take a look at an example of a functional résumé.

Sample of a Functional Résumé

Name

City, State   **E-mail address**   **Phone**

Executive Administrator: A highly motivated and effective professional, proficient in corporate administration, office management and cross-functional collaboration. Superior communication and organizational skills with a demonstrated talent for developing and managing multiple projects and programs. Experience includes domestic and international support.

KEY SKILLS & ACCOMPLISHMENTS

Executive Administration

- Provided executive-level support to senior executive of a worldwide sales operation, ensuring maximum effectiveness and productivity for all operations.
- Concurrently supported six separate organizations, facilitating cross-collaboration and increased program visibility for each.

- Developed communication materials that informed, educated, and disseminated valuable information and increased sales for a global sales organization.
- Designed and maintained customer, vendor and supplier databases that resulted in readily available and current information.

Project Management

- Coordinated and tracked training and development project for international sales team, including instruction on Web-based tools, resulting in more effective management of employees.
- Collaborated with corporate team and systems engineers to develop and initiate methodology for assessing "walk away value" of employees and improving retention. Maintained ongoing responsibility for retaining and managing data.
- Achieved recognition for successful completion of yearlong project involving implementation of Management Access Tools (MAT) that ensured managers current information on retaining staff. Collaborated with engineering, human resources, IT and technical operations.
- Developed and implemented membership drives, events and marketing programs that increased association's revenue and membership 25%.
- Administered large commercial leasing projects. Successfully recruited tenants and effectively negotiated contracts that ensured 33% initial pre-leasing.

Event and Meeting Planning

- Managed domestic and international travel, transportation, accommodations and entertainment for senior executives.
- Organized quarterly business review meetings to track and analyze organizational business plans and ensure goals and commitments were met.
- Maintained schedules, materials and logistical details to assist corporate managers with major speaking engagements and presentations targeted to increase industry-wide recognition.
- Planned and coordinated open houses and groundbreaking ceremonies to showcase products and services of a large real estate company.

PROFESSIONAL EXPERIENCE

Sun Systems, Seattle, Washington   2006—Present
Executive Administrator, Worldwide Operations

Seattle Advantage, Seattle, Washington   2003—2006
Executive Administrator/Office Manager

Residential Builders Cooperative, Seattle, Washington   1998—2003
Membership Director

Hemisphere Corporation, Seattle, Washington   1990—1998
Marketing Manager

EDUCATION

Human Resources Associate Certification, Lake Washington College, Kirkland, WA

Licensed Real Estate Broker, State of Washington

COMPUTER SKILLS

Microsoft Word, Excel, Outlook, PowerPoint, Access, Publisher, Visio, Photoshop, Adobe Acrobat

---

The overall goal is to prepare a résumé that looks good, is easy to read and that represents you as an accomplished professional, who can solve problems or meet specific needs for the Hiring Manager.

Positioning Yourself

The job seeker, who is disciplined and professional in his approach, will understand that "positioning" himself in his audience's mind is the focus of everything he includes in his résumés and cover letters, and is an integral part of "branding." That's why he clearly and concisely shows that he/she:

- Understands at least some of the needs of the Hiring Manager and his company.

- Explains what he/she has to offer and illustrates why this is valuable to the Hiring Manager and his company.

This usually takes place in an objective statement (or headline) that targets the specific position the job seeker is seeking. Then, in a *Career Summary,* you sell your specific skills in a way that benefits that particular company and defines your strongest competencies as a means for the company to achieve greater results.

Your résumé is not a statement about what you want from the company. It's a statement about what you have to give to the company to assist it in reaching its goals.

Present your skills and accomplishments in a descriptive and compelling way to gain the attention you deserve. Use action words—words that jump off the paper to gain the Hiring Manager's attention. Download a free list of powerful action words from our website at www.TheCareer-Suite.com/actionwords.

Design—An Integral Part

As with an ad, your résumé has about five to ten seconds to attract and hold the attention of the Hiring Manager. If it achieves that, you probably have another ten to fifteen seconds to present your experience, qualifications, and especially, your accomplishments—the results from your efforts. This is where you sell, sell, sell! Turn all your "features" into benefits for the Hiring Manager and his company.

You need to accomplish a lot of things in this ten to fifteen second window on no more than two pages. As you construct your résumé, keep these seven questions in mind:

1. What do I know about the Hiring Manager's needs that makes me a good fit for his company?

2. What makes me and my experience unique or stand out from other job seekers?

3. What do Hiring Managers need and want to know about me that will interest them in talking to me?

4. How can I prove, to Hiring Managers, that I can add value and contribute to their success?

5. What results have I accomplished for my past employers?

6. How can I state my accomplishments without bragging or appearing conceited?

7. And finally, how do I avoid having my résumé screened out of the job search before it gets to the Hiring Manager?

Your résumé and cover letter should demonstrate that you understand and are responding directly to the company's specific needs and opportunities. Again, this is where your research on the company and the requirements of the job comes into play. Match your résumé and cover letter to the posted job requirements and company needs.

To successfully land the job you want, take advantage of every opportunity to tell your story. This includes a well-written cover letter and résumé.

A great place to find job postings and their requirements is on company websites. You can also find out information about the company culture, values, products, and sometimes, their future plans and some of their challenges, so a company website is always a good place to start your research about a job.

And finally, show your personality as well as your accomplishments in your résumés and cover letters. Yes, these are business communications, but that does not mean colorless. Speak to the recipient one-on-one as you would in a conversation—after all, that's what you want—a conversation with him! Speak from your heart to reach his.

Remember Your Résumé Is

- Your written sales pitch to your potential customer.

- A sales or marketing "brochure" that describes the benefits of a valuable product (you) that can be a strong addition to the Hiring Manager's team and company.

- A keeper, not something that is tossed into the "round file."

A résumé will serve you well, especially, when combined with a strong, targeted cover letter.

THE PURPOSE OF A COVER LETTER

There are differing opinions about cover letters. Some people even say they're not needed. This is a myth! They are most definitely necessary!

Any number of people may be handling your cover letter and résumé. Their goal is to move it forward or eliminate it. You can't be sure how they make that decision. An initial screener usually looks for the specific job you are seeking and how your qualifications meet the requirements for the job. The Hiring Managers and interviewers will likely try to get a feel for your personality and your true interest in their company. They may read the letter first or after the résumé, if the résumé is of interest— or not at all, but still an appropriate cover letter is expected.

From your standpoint, you want to make certain you take advantage of every opportunity to tell your story—why you are a good fit for a company. The cover letter provides an opportunity to tell the Hiring Manager that you have specifically chosen them and explain why. This is important because it shows them that you aren't just randomly sending out résumés and cover letters across your industry. It also provides another opportunity to promote your candidacy for the job and to position yourself as standing out from the crowd of other job seekers.

Keep the tone of your cover letter professional, not chummy or personal.

When composing your cover letters, keep these basic points in mind:

- Use the same style as your résumé—same font, same stationery, if it is to be sent in the regular mail. The cover letter and résumé need to look like they go together.

- Limit the letter to one page and three to four paragraphs.

- Make it look easy and inviting to read. Create some white space.

- Don't make your cover letter read like a form letter that goes to everyone.

- Keep the tone and content professional—no jokes!

- Keep it career-related—no personal stories.

- Place the important information "above the fold"—at the top of the letter.

Remember that your cover letter is part of your brand and a strong marketing tool that must be designed to appeal to the needs of the Hiring Manager and his company.

Additional Cover Letter Review Suggestions

- Check for "I," "me" and "my" words. Using them too frequently gives the impression that your letter may be focused too much on *your* interests rather than the needs of the *Hiring Manager* and his company.

- Edit for content and clarity:

  ○ Is your message clear and does it support the purpose of the letter?

  ○ If someone reads only the first sentence of each paragraph, would they understand your basic message?

- Check for repetition and revise or condense.

- Check to see that it is easy to read. Try varied sentence lengths. Break up very long sentences. Use short sentences for emphasis.

- Check for missing information and the overall appearance of your letter.

- Once you have drafted a good, solid cover letter, use it to format and customize for each job you apply for.

- Follow-up. Don't be a pest, but do follow up with the Hiring Manager so that he knows you are interested.

- And *always* thoroughly proof read.

Remember what we said was the most insightful comment we heard from respondent Hiring Managers about résumés: "If you don't put forth the effort to make your résumé look as good as possible, why would a Hiring Manager expect you to put forth the effort to do your best on the job?"

That comment is on target not only for résumés, but also for cover letters; in fact, your best effort is necessary for all printed materials, as well as your face-to-face marketing! Never forget it. Incorporate it into everything you do in your job search and you'll land the job you want faster and with less stress.

A Few Words Regarding References

The main purpose of references is to provide your prospective Hiring Manager and company the wherewithal to verify the authenticity of what you claim: how you contributed to the success of former employers, your professional reputation, and whether you are a worry free employee—or if you *aren't*! So, it is imperative that your résumé references can relate your message effectively and with integrity.

It is true that some companies only check references after hiring; others don't check them at all. Regardless of how your prospective employer handles your references, it is still important that both you and your references are prepared. Consider the following in preparing your reference list and distributing it:

- Choose the right references
- Contact and preparing your references
- Keep your references informed
- Know when to present your references

CHOOSE THE *RIGHT* REFERENCES

You need to be sure that the people you ask to provide a reference for you know the quality of your work and the value you brought to the orga-nizations you worked for. Be sure you are confident that the manner in which a refer-ence discusses you will be positive.

It is imperative that your references can relate your message effectively and with integrity. So, job seekers must choose them carefully and keep them informed—especially when a Hiring Manager may want to contact them.

Identify eight to twelve positive ref-erences. Work to achieve a mixture of individuals, so you can match the appro-priate reference for each job opportunity. A combination of former bosses, colleagues, people who worked for you, senior execu-tives who know your work, team project members, vendors, customers, and others outside work can offer a well-rounded affir-mation of your value to an organization. But keep in mind, you will usually provide only three to four references when asked.

And be sure *not* to include your references on your résumé. Pre-pare a separate reference list document that you can present when they are requested. And be sure to provide references only when asked. This saves you and your references time and effort.

Note: If you leave your current boss off the list, be prepared to explain why, but only if asked. If you aren't asked, don't mention it.

How To Contact and Prepare Your References

Before you add someone to your reference list, contact them and ask if they would be willing to give you a *positive* reference if a prospective employer called them about you. Be sure to tell your reference what kind of job you are seeking and send them a copy of your résumé.

Keeping Your References Informed

When asked to provide your references, you should immediately call the ones you are going to provide to the Hiring Manager and let them know that they may be contacted and who will be contacting them. And be sure to ask your references to follow-up with you, if and when they are contacted.

If you haven't already done so, send them an up-to-date résumé and a copy of the cover letter you sent to that Hiring Manager. Coach your references on what skills and accomplishments are important to highlight in their conversation with the Hiring Manager. And be sure to ask your references to follow-up with you, if and when they are contacted.

Two Final Important Points Often Overlooked

- If your name has changed since you worked with a reference, be sure to let them know your current name.

- Your references should also be considered part of your networking team and treated in that manner (Learn more about this in the next secret).

Summary

Basically, there really are only two effective ways for a job seeker to contact a Hiring Manager and gain a face-to-face interview:

- Providing him with a dynamite résumé and cover letter that speaks directly to the job requirements and the needs of the organization and makes the Hiring Manager stop and take notice.

- Attain a referral to the Hiring Manager from a trusted acquaintance—yours and theirs.

The purpose of a job résumé is really to accomplish two main objectives:

1. Represent you in the best light when you can't do so in person.

2. Create enough interest in the mind of the Hiring Manger, or the person who reviews résumés for them, so that they offer you an exploratory interview and an interview for a specific job opening.

The purpose of a cover letter:

- Provides an opportunity to tell the Hiring Manager that you have specifically chosen them and explain why.

- Shows them that you aren't just randomly sending out résumés and cover letters across your industry.

- Provides another opportunity to promote your candidacy for the job and to position yourself as standing out from the crowd of other job seekers.

- Your job experience, education, background, career objectives and summary statements should be uniquely targeted to an audience "of one" in a specific company and industry.

- Clearly and concisely explain what you have to offer and illustrate why this is valuable to the Hiring Manager and his company.

Your résumé and cover letter are *not* statements about what you *want from* the company. They are statements about what you have to *give to* the company to assist it in reaching its goals.

NETWORK YOUR WAY INTO THE HIDDEN JOB MARKET

Success Story

This success story is actually from our personal experience and shows how and why networking is so easy, as well as effective. Read how Eleanor's experience helped a client with another aspect of his job search.

"I've had the pleasure of helping many people get jobs, and not just by hiring them! I have a broad and deep network (and so do you). It is not uncommon for people I know to ask me to refer people they know to someone else I know.

"Once, when I was helping a client prepare a résumé, I mentioned how important it is to network to ensure the success of a job search. After we finished our conversation, there was a lull as I waited for him to "pop the question," but he didn't. So, I finally asked him, "Are you going to take advantage of the opportunity staring you in the face to network? What about asking me if I know anyone that you might talk to about your job search?"

I started to laugh and he did too. Then, he said somewhat skeptically, "Okay, do you know anyone that might be willing to talk to me about commercial real estate training and job opportunities?"

I quickly responded, "Why, yes I do!" Long story short, I got my client in touch with my friend at a highly respected real estate firm. He was hired into their intern-training program and now has a successful career in commercial real estate!

Don't ever fool yourself into thinking that you don't have a big enough network! It can and should get larger every day as you simply talk to people. Everyone you encounter in your day, in person, over the phone, in e-mail, wherever, is a potential connection to someone who can help you in your job search.

Remember: One of the best things about networking, besides getting an introduction to someone who may be your next employer, is that people really like to help people. So, don't hesitate to be direct with them and specifically ask for help and discover just how effective networking can be for you.

Where the Jobs Are

You've probably heard it said that it's not so much what you know, but *who* you know. That applies especially to the job seeker. More than seventy-five percent of all available jobs are unadvertised and, therefore, hidden from the average job seeker. Networking opens the door wide to the hidden job market for a job seeker.

You can only find out about these jobs through someone who knows about the job opening—through word of mouth, and word of mouth means networking. The result is a referral—the Holy Grail for a job seeker.

Quotes from Hiring Managers Regarding Referrals (Networking for Candidates)

"It's unlikely that I would be able to take the time to interview unless I had a specific need. However, and this is the most crucial point, if a person comes recommended from a trusted friend or even trusted 'acquaintance', I will take the time to interview. A recommendation, telephone call, e-mail from someone I know trumps almost every other issue. Hiring is somewhat of a crapshoot, especially for the small business owner. Consequently, a personal reference invariably puts a candidate to the 'top of the pile'."

"With so many persons looking for work, the best thing is to try to get someone 'on the inside' or someone who knows somebody on the inside to intervene on your behalf. Network, like heck, to try to identify that individual."

"The best way I learned to get interviews is through 'people I know'. Do not ask them for a job or an interview, but ask them if they know anyone at specific companies you are targeting, or if they know

of anyone who may be looking for someone with your capabilities. Work your friends and business contacts to find network contacts."

"Getting the interview requires a personal recommendation either from a screener or someone I know or respect. I've given up doing first interviews."

Get the Right People to Make the Right Comments to the Right Hiring Managers

In other words, network your way into the hidden job market and the company you want to work for.

Networking has been defined as the art of building relationships and alliances. What does that mean for your job search? Well, here's what it does *not* mean: simply asking people for a job or if they know someone who is hiring! It does *not* mean contacting everyone you know when you are looking for a new job and asking if they know someone who's hiring.

If accomplished with forethought and wisdom, it *does* mean building relationships to last way beyond your immediate job search activities. Networking actually begins long before a job search and you probably don't even realize you are doing it. Finally, it has been consistently cited as the number one way to get a new job.

Overwhelming evidence supports the fact that the best jobs never get posted or advertised. In fact, studies have shown that between seventy-five to ninety percent of all available jobs are only found in this "hidden job market" by referral. You need to find ways to get referred into this hidden job market, if you want to be where these jobs are.

Almost every Hiring Manager we interviewed said networking was the best way to get on their calendar—even when they don't have an open position to fill. So, networking should be at the top of every job seeker's list of valuable tools. Regardless, if you think you know the right people or not, time and again, it has been proven that someone you do know, knows someone you should know. Networking, done the right way, uncovers dozens of hidden resources of influential people who can and are willing to help you.

NETWORKING—A JOB SEEKER'S TOP PRIORITY

Job seekers who network can reach 75% more job openings in their job search than non-networking job seekers! Which are you?

The Hiring Managers, we spoke to, said that a referral by a trusted third party is the best introduction for a job seeker. Without exception, all of them told us they would see a job seeker who had been referred to them. And networking is the quickest way to get you that introduction. This should be no surprise. Everyone talks about networking. The surprise is how many job seekers don't do it or don't do it effectively.

A third party referral immediately builds your credibility due to the "halo" effect. If the referring person is trusted, the job seeker being referred by them is looked on as trustworthy also. And people want to do business with people they trust. It's kind of like using a trusted spokesperson in an ad talking about the benefits of a product. Because you trust the spokesperson, you may consider trying the product. The Hiring Manager trusts your networking contact, so he will have an open mind and probably a positive expectation about you. And now, you have an open door to the hidden job market!

NETWORKING—THE COST AND TIME SAVINGS ADVANTAGE

Hiring Managers also told us that networking can save a company considerable cost and effort in advertising a position and sorting through all the résumés, cover letters and phone calls of the hundreds of job seekers who respond to their advertising.

We are not discounting the value of résumés and cover letters or other forms of initial contact here. They have significant value. However, you need to know that networking can greatly magnify the impact of those documents. Hiring Managers also told us that they are doing less advertising because it just isn't as effective as it was years ago: "…too many applicants responding to ads don't even meet the basic job requirements."

Another huge benefit to networking is getting to know people inside a company you are interested in—even if they aren't hiring at that time. If they get to know you now, when a position opens up, you already have a contact to reconnect with inside.

Networking is also consistently cited as the number one way to win the job. *The 2008 Sources of Hire* study conducted by the consulting firm Career Xroads interviewed forty-nine firms with a total of more than a million employees. Internal transfers and promotions constituted thirty percent of all the positions these companies filled. These transfers and promotions usually leave an open position behind. Networking enables job seekers to find out about these hidden, open positions that often don't get advertised. When you or anyone else hears of a promotion or transfer, the next thought should be, "Gee, who's filling the job they left behind?"

NETWORKING—A GROWING TREND FOR THE FORESEEABLE FUTURE

Networking is vital to the successful job seeker and will only become more important in the future.

Some of the best places to go to network include:

- Professional Conferences.
- Seminars.
- Conventions.
- Professional Organizations.
- Volunteer Events /Charity Events.
- Fundraisers.

If you think you don't know many Network Prospects, go to www.TheCareerSuite.com/expandyournetwork and learn more about how to quickly and effectively find people who are willing to help you in your job search.

SOCIAL NETWORKS FROM A JOB SEARCH PERSPECTIVE

A blog is a perfect "space" to build and expand upon your "brand" when you use it professionally.

There is a growing trend in adapting social networks for job search purposes. It is becoming more evident that using social networks wisely allows all parties involved to more efficiently and effectively search for and reach their target employer/employee. The most important point for job seekers to remember about social networks is, when you use them as part of your job search marketing, they are *not social*. They're *professional networks*. Be selective in choosing and using social networks. And above all, understand what each can and cannot do for you.

The Top Three

No surprises here: the top social networks, especially useful in a job search, include LinkedIn, Twitter and Facebook, with the relatively new Google+ coming in a close fourth. One of the best features of the above sites is that they are free, easy to join and simple to use. On them, you will find a multitude of opportunities to connect with career and job search experts and companies that are hiring. You'll also find the sharing aspects with other job seekers a useful tool.

The Benefits and Pitfalls of Social Networking for Job Search Purposes

The most valuable benefit of social networking is being able to rapidly and easily reach more individuals who may be able to help you in your job search. The biggest pitfall: you run the risk of hurting your chances with an employer if you use it incorrectly and unprofessionally, or if you don't double check the information you find while "chatting" with others on these sites.

Here are ten basic tips to keep you on a "winning streak" to successfully use social networking in your job search:

1. Make it easy for potential employers to find you online and make it professional and presentable.

2. Establish a professional profile that you use solely for communicating with business contacts and companies that interest you. Use your full name for your user name. It's far more professional than something witty you would use for communicating with your friends.

3. If possible, use a professional portrait for the photo you post. Keep in mind you want to appear professional and friendly.

4. Build your "brand." Showcase your skills and experience. Use it to help portray you in a professional light. This provides potential employers with a strong perception of you as the job candidate to go to when hiring.

5. Post updates to let potential employers and colleagues know about you and your progress in your job search. Keep it positive and upbeat.

6. Do not speak badly about a previous employer or one you're interested in working for.

7. Maintain a professional demeanor with every aspect of your professional (social) network.

8. Post your résumé, so that anyone interested in hiring you can access it easily. You might consider using a blog for this purpose as well. Remember to track where you have posted your résumé (along with your user name and password).

9. Protect your privacy. Set up accounts just for the purpose of your job search and do *not* include *any* personal information. For instance, use a dedicated email address for your job search. This will serve two purposes. 1) It protects your privacy and 2) it helps you track your job search applications and correspondence.

    Also use a login name and password that's unique to this account.

Check out companies that contact you. One easy way to do this is a basic Google check of the company. Another useful search is to Google the company name using the descriptor "scam" or "reviews." Example: XYZ Company scam or XYZ Company reviews.

10. Finally, Google your own name and check what's being said about you online. Remember, there is a ton of information available. Even your social tweets show up on Google! And it's exceptionally easy for a potential employer to find information you may have preferred to remain private.

Networking Opportunities Abound

By now, you should realize that networking does not have to be a stressful, planned and choreographed event. Opportunities to network are everywhere. You simply have to open your mind to the possibilities. Think of this—you are networking even when you are at a neighbor's backyard barbeque. So relax! Quite often, the networking opportunity will present itself to you if you just open yourself up to the idea.

Summary

More than seventy-five percent of all available jobs are unadvertised and, therefore, hidden from the average job seeker. Networking opens the door wide to the hidden job market for a job seeker. Networking, done the right way, uncovers dozens of hidden resources of influential people, who can and *are willing*, to help you.

The result is a referral—the Holy Grail for a job seeker. Hiring Managers said that a referral by a trusted third party is the best introduction for a job seeker. Without exception, all told us they would see a job seeker who had been referred to them.

The benefits of networking for the *candidate*:

- Consistently cited as the number one way to win the job.
- Sets the stage for your résumés and cover letters.
- Introduces you to people within the company you're interested in.

The benefits of networking for the *company*:

- Saves considerable cost and effort in advertising a position and sorting through all the résumés, cover letters and phone calls of the hundreds of job seekers who respond to their advertising.

- Companies are doing less advertising of job openings because it just isn't as effective as it was years ago. "Too many responses to ads don't even meet the basic job requirements."

There appears to be a growing trend in adapting social networks for job search purposes

Finally, networking does not have to be a stressful, planned and choreographed event. It can take place anywhere with almost anybody.

Secret 5:

ANNIHILATE JOB INTERVIEW WEAKNESSES AND WIN THE JOB YOU WANT

Success Story

Tracy had been seeking employment for several months after moving to Florida. She had sent out résumés and received a few invitations to interview. But, even after what she felt was a successful interview, she never received a call back.

She became confused and frustrated because she truly felt she had the experience and skills those companies said they needed. She kept asking herself, "What am I doing wrong? Is every other candidate for these jobs always so much more qualified than I am?"

She then began reading our secret on résumés and this one on overcoming job interview weaknesses.

Here's what she said, after her very next interview, "I thought I was prepared for a job interview before I read your chapter on it. Boy was I mistaken! I saw that I didn't know all the kinds of questions I needed to have answers for. I also didn't realize that when asked if I had any questions, I really needed to be prepared with some, and how doing so would help a Hiring Manager see me as a good fit for his company.

What I appreciated most was the idea of developing success stories to share with an interviewer when he asked about my experience and achievements. This was a Godsend. These stories helped me clarify, for myself, as much as for the interviewer, what I had not only accomplished, but what I truly have to offer a potential employer. I never felt so confident in an interview before and so connected to the interviewer and his company."

It was after a couple more interviews that Tracy emailed to say she had received a great job offer!

Remember: what's really important here is that Tracy's successful interviewing experience can be yours, just as easily. Tracy is not an exception to the rule and neither are you. All it takes is knowing what to do, how to do it and practice, practice, practice. After all, who has more of a vested interest in your success than you?

Time to Show Your Stuff

So far, you've developed and are using a smart job search marketing strategy. You've impressed the heck out of your networking contacts and got an introduction to a Hiring Manager in a company of interest. You've developed marketing materials such as your résumé and cover letter, customized to meet the company's needs. You've won an interview and now you need to get ready to meet the Hiring Manager to show him your stuff. This is your face-to-face opportunity to convert strangers into raving fans—and you can do it!

Remember that the entire interview process is a step-by-step method of whittling lots of candidates down to one, systematically screening people out of the interview process to find the one candidate who best meets the needs of the company and the Hiring Manager. Your goal is to avoid being screened out along the way, so you have the opportunity to represent yourself in person.

The interview is where you proceed from pre-sell to sell. In marketing terms—the successful networking you've done, along with your targeted résumés and cover letters pre-sold you to the Hiring Manager, opened the door of opportunity. The interview is where the well-prepared and confident job seeker—*you*—makes the sale. You have successfully been screened into the next step of the interview process. Congratulations!

Quotes From a Few Hiring Managers on Making a Positive Impression

"Good communications skills are a must; they need to express themselves concisely and be able to easily explain what they can do. They

need to quickly make a connection with me and be at ease with themselves. So, smile as appropriate. And they need to focus on what they can offer and not what they need from us."

"Let me put it this way:

- *Confidence, but not arrogance.*
- *Genuine interest, not just looking for a job.*
- *Communication skills.*
- *Knowledge of the company and position.*
- *Impressive qualifications, references, skills.*
- *Something unique, e.g., background, skill set, accomplishments, outside activities, etc."*

"I am looking for cogent explanations of career history including ability to describe the business conditions, the challenges associated with the role, how they approached it and why, and the outcomes. I am similarly looking to see if everything hangs together, whether they faced challenges that they powered through successfully."

"First and foremost, I'm hoping to 'connect' with the applicant in some way. A 'BS' artist is a non-starter. I can remember flying a candidate for a vice president of operations position into town for an interview. Within four minutes, he had told me several times how valuable he was and how bad his previous company was. I terminated the interview right then and sent him back to the airport. As you might expect, he was very surprised as was the headhunter who set up the interview with me. The point is, whether the interviewer is as abrupt as I was in this instance, very often the interview is over before it really starts when all someone sees are his own issues."

"What I'm looking for is sincerity, friendliness and an ability to listen! Also, an ability to be succinct, but not reticent, in addition to, ability and experience."

Expect the Unexpected

As is evidenced in the above quotes, you need to expect the unexpected as well as the expected in an interview. Which means, as in every other aspect of your job search, you need to prepare for the interview. You need to become very familiar with the latest events and issues in the industry, what's happening with the company you're interested in, and with the Hiring Manager. Most of all, you need to understand how to match what you've accomplished to what the company and Hiring Manager needs, if you truly want to make a positive impression. More than almost anything else, this will set you apart from the crowd of other job seekers applying for the same job.

You must be comfortable with what you have to offer the company and how you're going to tell your story in terms of the company's needs and opportunities. Remember, this is your best opportunity to establish that your experience, talents and accomplishments would be beneficial to the company and Hiring Manager. So, spend time prior to an interview preparing for it.

Truism: The job seeker, who wins in the interview, wins the job and the job seeker, who wins the job, wins in the interview. So be prepared!

Tips: Preparing for an Interview

- Make a list of your attributes.

- Think about what you can offer the Hiring Manager.

- Be prepared to respond to the unexpected, such as, "What's something that has been a problem for you at work?"

- Know how to speak to your faults as well as your virtues. Know how to turn them into "lessons learned."

- Then rehearse, rehearse, rehearse!

PROFESSIONAL VS AMATEUR INTERVIEWERS

Another interviewing consideration is who is interviewing you. Generally, there are two kinds of interviewers—the professional and the amateur.

The *professional* is someone who interviews people as a key or core part of their job, like search consultants and human resource professionals. They are usually trained and highly skilled in effective questioning and usually prepare specific questions for the interview after having discussed and researched the open position with the Hiring Manager or company contact (in the case of the search professional). They will be prepared and keep the interview focused and on track. They will probably ask a lot of different types of questions, so listen carefully and answer concisely, directly, and with specifics.

The *amateur* is a person who is interviewing candidates to fill a specific job and probably doesn't do a lot of interviewing, unless the job has high turnover. (Many entry level jobs have high turnover because of promotions—a good thing, or because they are temporary jobs, as in an actor's working as waiters, etc.) Some of these interviewers are great, but some are not. They often take a more general approach and many will ask you something like, "Tell me about yourself." This isn't a bad question. It just isn't very specific and can lead you to giving a long, unfocused answer. You need to be prepared with a concise and relevant response. They don't want to hear your life story. Don't volunteer a lot of information unless it is focused and a true selling point for your candidacy for the job.

Don't mistake the label of *amateur* as unimportant or inferior. These are the people who have the power to make you an offer—the professionals usually don't. The amateur just isn't as practiced in interviewing and may feel as uncomfortable as you do in the situation. Many Hiring Managers who interview, however, have made it a point to become excellent interviewers, so don't make assumptions that they aren't.

Practice Practice Practice

Don't try to "wing it," if you're sincerely interested in getting the job. Practice your answers (out loud, with a friend or family member) to potential questions that might be asked.

Yes, your answers should sound spontaneous, but practice builds confidence and reduces the possibilities of uncomfortable, long pauses caused by the need to "think on your feet" about an answer.

Taking a moment to think is fine, but overly long pauses makes it seem, to the Hiring Manager, that you're unprepared, or worse, that you are making up an answer. Tailor your success stories to the specific job requirements and the research you've done on the company. Be prepared with specific examples of your accomplishments, answers to possible unusual questions and relevant knowledge about the Hiring Manager and his company.

Then, you appear to be what you are—informed and intelligent. By the way, you should also use the information you gathered from your research to help you make a decision, if you are offered a job.

STANDARD INTERVIEW QUESTIONS YOU SHOULD EXPECT TO BE ASKED

- Tell me about a project that you are proud of. "Tell me about..." questions are the best kind of interview questions and get asked a lot.

   Be prepared with success stories that show the value you have contributed to your employers in your career. Be succinct. Don't ramble. Tell the situation, what problems you overcame, what actions you took and the results.

- What would your former boss say about you?

   A question like this is best answered with the skills, traits and qualities that you know are needed in the new position. Support them with examples. "My former boss said that I was particularly talented in investigating and analyzing a problem. The first time I remember she mentioned this was when we had an equipment failure that no one could fix. I spent several days observing the entire operation and was able to pinpoint the phase of the process that was causing the problem. It saved us countless man hours and downtime expense."

- Are you creative? Have you ever fired anyone? Have you ever led a project?

  Lots of questions like this are a one-two punch. You answer, "Yes." Then the interviewer follows up with…

- What makes you think you are creative? Or, tell me about the situation.

  Now you need to be ready with a good success story again.

- Why should I hire you?

  The best answer to this is to inform them about your background, experience and how it fits perfectly with the requirements of the job you are interviewing for. You need to explain this and make a case for what a great fit you are for the job.

- What did you like best about your last job?

  Again, lead the interviewer to see that what you enjoyed—and are an expert at delivering—fits perfectly with what they are looking for.

- Where do you want to be in five years?

  This isn't a great question, but it gets asked—a lot! A good answer is, "I would expect that I would have made significant contributions to the company and that I would either have the privilege of more responsibility or promotion because of it."

Some of the Trickier Interview Questions You Might Have To Face Are

- What is your greatest weakness?

  Always answer with something insignificant to the position you are seeking.

  (Example: "I don't like speaking to large crowds," when you are applying to be a graphic artist.) or something that you have over-come (Example: "I used to have difficulty in giving feedback to people who work for me, but when I realized how much it positively impacted their performance, I find it's easy and the people I work with have said they appreciate it also. It can still be difficult, but I know the result will be worth it.")

- Tell me about a time you failed in a project.

  Never admit to failure, but you can give an example of how you learned from a difficult project and successfully applied the learning to your future performance.

- What do you worry about?

  Reframe negative questions like this. "I wouldn't say that I worry, but I do focus a lot of my thinking on…as I know how critical it is to the success of the company."

- After describing a difficult situation, the interviewer asks, "How would you handle that?"

  When asked general or hypothetical questions, it is best to try to relate the situation to a real life situation you have successfully resolved. You could respond by saying, "I experienced a situation somewhat similar to the one you described, maybe that would be a good way to show you how I have handled difficult situations in the past." Then tell your story in no more than two to three minutes, describing the situation, the problems you faced, what actions you took and then the positive results you got.

- I know the company you used to work for is developing a new snack food product for market. Can you tell me about it?

  If you are ever asked to reveal confidential information of any sort—don't do it! In most cases, the interviewer isn't really looking for the secret; they want to know how you handle sensitive information. Just say, "Unfortunately, that information is still considered confidential and I wouldn't feel comfortable passing it along."

- How old are you? Where were you born? Do you go to church?

  Some inexperienced interviewers are unaware that questions like these are not good to ask and if they use the answers to screen you out of the interview process, it could be considered a violation of Federal laws prohibiting job discrimination. Your best answer to questions like these is a question. "Is age a concern for this position?" "Can you tell me how where I was born is related to this job?" "Does going to church have a bearing on this job?" Ask the question for clarification; you don't want to appear evasive or embarrass the interviewer, but using this technique can keep the interview focused on the job requirements and not on issues that should not be considered in the selection process.

After you feel comfortable with your answers to possible questions the *Hiring Manager* may ask, think about the questions *you* should ask him about the company and the open position you're applying for. Ask insightful questions about the company based on your research. Ask questions that show your interest in the job and enthusiasm for the company.

In other words, *be prepared.*

TWO NEVER FAIL QUESTIONS YOU CAN ASK AN INTERVIEWER

- What do you see as the most important skills and qualities required for someone to succeed in this position at your company?

- Over the next six (could be nine or twelve) months, what would you like to see accomplished by the person you hire in this position?

Make a Good First Impression

Pay attention to details like your personal appearance, punctuality, and demeanor. Know the hidden interview details that can trip up any interview, like when an interview *really* begins. (Hint: it's when you leave your home the morning of the interview, not when you're shaking hands with the Hiring Manager.) Know the hidden secrets of looking the part. (Hint: *ask* the dress code before the interview, but if you can't—very few applicants have lost an offer because they presented themselves as a professional.) Know the secret of a good entrance. (Hint: make sure you arrive on time, not more than three to five minutes early and *never, ever late!*)

You may think that if you have the best answers to interview questions, you'll get a job offer. What you say *is* critically important, but that isn't the only factor in making an impression that will win you the job.

Research shows that there are many factors that influence people about who we are, what we can do, and whether they want to have us on their team. You experience this in your life every day. To prove this, take a trip to the grocery store or a mall and be observant of the people around you. Take note of the impressions they make on you about their education, prosperity, intelligence, personality, and so on—just by the way they present themselves to the world. Appearances is powerful stuff, so you need to take full advantage of it and make the best one you know how to.

Think About the Message You Want To Send and Then Look Like It

Remember, first impressions are lasting impressions! You want to walk in looking and sounding like the brand message you want to send. That is the image you want the Hiring Manager to have impressed in memory. Don't look like a brand that doesn't match the words of the message you are sending in the interview. If your look and sound don't sync, it is distracting and unauthentic. It won't get you the job! When practicing for an interview, have someone watch your nonverbal communications as well as your other interviewing skills. It could be what clinches the job offer for you.

WHAT'S THE PURPOSE OF YOUR INTERVIEW

Know the hidden stumbling blocks on interviewing. (Hint: Understand the type of interview you will be participating in.) And speaking of interview types, there are at least five different types of interviews and each is used for a different purpose. When you're invited to interview with a company, don't be hesitant to ask what type of an interview it will be. In fact, the Hiring Manager may very well be impressed that you recognize there are different types.

THE TYPES OF INTERVIEWS

The screening interview. Its purpose is generally to verify information in your résumé and to find out if you meet the minimum qualifications for the job. This, quite often, is done with a telephone call.

The group interview. A Hiring Manager generally meets with several candidates at one time to determine who are leaders or followers, and to learn who is a "team player.

The panel interview. This is used to interview a candidate by several people and may be somewhat intimidating, but provides a concentrated effort to gather individual and collective impressions of the candidate.

The candidate who is prepared for any type of interview is a stand out in the crowd of job seekers.

The stress interview. Its purpose is generally to weed out candidates who can't handle adversity or a stressful environment.

The selection interview. The one every job seeker wants to get to; its purpose is to verify you have the qualifications for the job and most importantly, if you will "fit in."

Tips: For a winning interview:

- Look the part—like you belong there.

- Establish rapport, build credibility and trust—maintain eye contact with a smile and relaxed facial expression.

- Find a mutual interest or take note of items of interest in the Hiring Manager's office.

- Listen attentively, and then after you listen, talk. Don't interrupt, or if you must, excuse yourself.

- Develop and use the skill to "read" people and their environment during the interview—*body language* is as important, and some-times more important, than what is spoken verbally. Take your cues from what the Hiring Manager says with body language as well as what he says.

- Bring up and respond to the needs you discovered about the orga-nization. *Emphasize* that you understand the importance of those needs. *Empathize* with the Hiring Manager regarding his desire to resolve problems and to make the most of the company's opportunities.

- Present yourself as a valuable *problem solver*—match your accom-plishments, experience and talents with what the company and the Hiring Manager need.

- Be ready to get an offer and get a job, even from companies that say they're not hiring.

- Know when to stop selling. This is one of the most important sales tactics you can use. Successful sales people will unanimously tell you that inexperienced sales people will lose more sales simply because they don't know when to stop.

- Don't be the first to mention compensation. Be truthful, but general in your response. You can always say that you are confident the salary will be commensurate with the responsibilities.

- Let the company make an offer regarding the compensation package. You are always appropriate in keeping the discussion focused on what you bring to the company, not what you want from it.

- Most of all, let the Hiring Manager know you are sincerely interested in joining an organization where you can be of value and contribute to making the whole team successful!

An Interview Evaluation or Take-Away

Once an interview is over, most Hiring Managers usually complete some kind of evaluation or assessment of your interview. This usually includes their opinion on how well you can fulfill the requirements of the job opening and how you will fit with their team.

You need to do the same thing after each job interview. Download a free "Interview Take-away" form at www. TheCareerSuite.com/interviewtakeaways to help you capture your impressions of the job, the Hiring Manager and anyone else you met. This is a valuable tool and can be extremely helpful to refer to later for follow-up, if you are asked back for second interviews, or if you get an offer.

Summary

The interview is your opportunity to make an effective connection with the Hiring Manager and probably a number of other individuals involved in the recruiting process. Effective preparation is requisite.

The recruiting and selection process is a step-by-step method of reducing many job seekers down to one—hopefully you.

- Your goal is to avoid being screened out along the way, so you can have a face-to-face meeting.

- The interview is when the well-prepared and confident job seeker makes the final sale that will result in an offer.

Expect the unexpected

- Know the latest events and issues in your industry and the company you are interest in.

- Know enough to match what you have accomplished in your career with the needs of the Hiring Manager and the company.

Professional vs. amateur interviewers

- Professionals interview people as a key or core part of their job. They will be well prepared and keep the interview focused and on track.

- Amateurs don't interview on a regular basis, but have the power to make the offer. Some are good interviewers and some are not, so you need to be a great interviewee to stay in the running.

Practice, practice, practice

- Practice sample interview questions and answers out loud with a friend to make your answers sound spontaneous and natural.

Standard questions you should expect to be asked and how to answer them

- There are standard or favorite questions many interviewers like to have answered and are proven to result in good information about job seekers and their abilities.

- Be prepared with stories and answers that tie your background and experience to the needs of the Hiring Manager and the company.

How to answer tricky, tough questions

- There are also favorite "trip up" questions to plan answers to before you go to an interview. These questions are often designed to try and reveal your weaknesses. You need to be prepared with positive responses to potential negative, illegal, or challenging questions.

Questions you should ask if given the opportunity

- Interviewers usually leave a few minutes for job seekers to ask questions. Be prepared with questions that will give you valuable information.

Secret 6:

FOLLOW-UP FOR SUCCESS— WIN THE JOB YOU WANT

Success Story

Hector is a vice president of talent acquisition for a large advertising agency. He had an open search for a Senior Level Art Director. He knew the ideal candidate needed to have more than just artistic capabilities. He or she would have to be able to lead and manage a very diverse and talented staff in four regional offices and also be able to satisfy the extraordinary demands for detail and follow through on their largest and most valuable client.

Hector felt like he had already "kissed" a lot of talented toads, but had not yet found his "prince or princess" who had the full capabilities of the job, until he found and interviewed fresh, energetic, and talented Ben. His portfolio of work spoke for itself. He clearly had the chops to assess the needs of a client's product and to create a compelling message and image of it to the consumer.

The big question was if Ben could lead other talented people, like himself, in a way that kept their creative juices flowing, but focused them on the demanding, specific and special needs of their clients.

Ben wanted this job and he knew from reading this secret, *Follow-up for Success—Win the Job You Want* and from his advertising career, how important it is to stay foremost in a customer's mind as he makes his "buying" decision. (This is called staying "top of mind" with a customer.) In this case, Hector was his customer.

Ben's strategy was to stay "top of mind" with Hector by "advertising" himself through tactful and thoughtfully placed follow-up messages over a period of several weeks. His follow through with Hector was impeccable! He started with a simple thank you to Hector, next he called to let Hector know of an article he found about their biggest client which pointed out a new direction they were considering in product development. He then sent the article to Hector.

He concluded his follow-up contact with Hector about three weeks after his interview with a letter restating his interest in the artistic director position, and he also mentioned that he would be willing to help Hector on a consulting interim basis while he concluded his search for the full time director, if Ben was not his top candidate.

Notice that in each follow-up, Ben was offering something of value to Hector and also indicating his continued interest in joining his company.

That was the clincher! Hector was so impressed with Ben's focus on detail, staying in touch, and being of help to him, that he picked up the phone and did what he was already inclined to do and offered Ben the job.

Hector told Ben that his professional follow-up had been helpful and it just proved that he was the kind of person they needed on their team.

Remember: Too many job seekers do not use this invaluable marketing tool or they use it ineffectively. This is just self-destructive. Enough said, now let's discuss how follow-up will work for you and why you should always— **always**—*follow up after an interview as part of a successful job search marketing plan.*

HOW YOU CAN STAY "UPPERMOST IN MIND" WITH THE HIRING MANAGER

Think about why successful sales people make follow-up calls with potential customers as part of their marketing plan. It gives them another opportunity to remind the potential customer of the benefits of his products, address any customer objections and show his interest and sincere concern about the customer's needs. And there's nothing better than a second chance to influence a potential customer.

Make Meaningful Follow-up Connections with Hiring Managers

Giving yourself a second opportunity to inform and reaffirm your value to a company and Hiring Manager is exactly the purpose in a job seeker's follow-up strategy and tactics. So far, you've used every appropriate tool to become top choice in the mind of a Hiring Manager and now you want to stay at the top with him—in the most positive way you can. A solid follow-up strategy will enable you to stand out from all other job seekers. This is true, first of all, because most of them will fail to do this; and second, they more than likely do not know how to do it effectively.

Listen To the Kind of Follow-Up That Appeals To Hiring Managers

"It's impressive when the job seeker writes a follow-up hand-written note after an interview that discusses something we talked about."

"I like an email from the job seeker because it is respectful and quick, but it should be more than a few lines (but not a novel!) If we talked about a specific idea and had a good conversation about it, a reference to it in the email is good."

"I like a note (handwritten is always best). I also like it if the job seeker follows up with information pertaining to something that came up in the interview, e.g, 'we talked about operating plans in our meeting—here's a plan I developed for XYZ that might give you a sense of my aptitude for that part of the job.'"

"I do appreciate an acknowledgement that the job seeker appreciated our time together. An email or handwritten note is fine…I don't care how the thank you comes; just that it does."

"I'm always impressed with a short handwritten note that arrives within forty-eight hours of the interview, e-mails are completely inappropriate for all, but the lowest level jobs."

"Everyone is now into sending e-mails after interviews. In the e-mail, showing a genuine interest in getting the job with our firm goes a long way."

And Here's What Annoys Them

"There's a fine line between a job seeker showing interest and coming across fake."

"Form letters or e-mails to all interviewers, follow-up phone calls for no apparent reason."

"Constant questions from the job seeker via phone or email are not appreciated."

"No-follow up or too much."

"A quick "form" e-mail is disappointing."

Three Important Points Are Evident From These Responses

1. A follow-up note is imperative and will help you stand out from the crowd.

2. You need to include information of value in the thank you note and customize it to the Hiring Manager with whom you interviewed and the conversation you had.

3. You need to discover, during your conversation with the Hiring Manager, what format your follow-up should take; e.g., a hand-written note, email, phone call, fax, etc.; what he considers appropriate. Advantages of each: E-mail—same day receipt as interview, within hours. Regular mail, (or fax) hand-written (or typed)—shows extra effort.

How you communicate with Hiring Managers in your job search is as important as what you say.

Our observation about how to reach a Hiring Manager—more experienced Hiring Managers seem to prefer the personal touch of a hand written note, while more junior or younger Hiring Managers lean toward email. Our best suggestion, ask the Hiring Manager how to best connect with him. Some senior executives still rely heavily on administrative support people to manage their correspondence, so unless otherwise directed, you may want to opt for regular mail with them to be sure your communications get into their physical inbox.

In any case, you should consider follow up as a vital part of your job search marketing strategy. It's a "must do" for the truly successful job seeker. As noted, it can serve as a strong competitive advantage over others who interviewed for the position, but didn't follow-up.

Ask the Hiring Manager, "I'd like to stay in touch with you about our meeting, would you prefer that I communicate through email, fax, or regular mail?"

Follow-Up and Follow-Thru in Your Job Search

- Always express appreciation for the interviewer's time and information.

- Be sure to provide a response to any requests from the interview.

- Consistently remind the interviewer how your strong points from your résumé/interview meet the company's needs.

Be Sure To Include These Points in Your Follow-Up Letter/Email

- Send a letter within twenty-four hours. Language should be businesslike. Send a separate, tailored letter to each individual who interviewed you. Prepare the letter in standard business format with their name, title, and address at the top. This can be hand written if short, but if it's a little longer (no more than one page), we suggest typewritten or email.

- Thank the interviewer for the opportunity to meet with him and refer to the company and the position.

- Refer to something discussed in the interview to build a mental bridge back to your specific interview.

- Include any additional information that shows you are qualified and a good fit for the position, or might reverse an objection that arose in the interview, or might solve a problem for the interviewer.

- Send anything you promised to share.

- Thank them for their courtesy and time.

- Tell them when you will follow up again.

Include Valuable Information in Follow-Up

It's important, in any follow-up, for job seekers to touch back with new, important information to a Hiring Manager. You might offer thoughts, ideas, suggestions, solutions, etc. for corporate issues raised during interview or other contact. Also think about offering economic or industry news related to your conversation.

Do not just send a standard "thank you for your time" letter or note. *Don't* rehash old news or harass the Hiring Manager by contacting him too often. Rehashing shrinks your credibility. Harassing—well you might as well shoot yourself in the foot, if you keep bothering him. As one Hiring Manager said, "Patience wins every time." Remember that sometimes the squeaky wheel doesn't get oiled, it gets thrown out.

Yes, there is a thin line between nothing, too little and too much. Nothing can be more helpful than following up with Hiring Managers appropriately and effectively. And nothing can be more disastrous to a job search than leaving this step out!

The following guidelines will help you determine the quantity of your follow-up contacts:

First follow-up—should happen immediately after the interview to say thank you; usually within forty-eight hours.

Second follow-up—a call within a week to ten days to ask about the position and to offer any additional information. Call sooner if the Hiring Manager lets you know he has a short timetable and needs to make a quick hiring decision.

Third follow-up—continue to follow up, especially if the employer asks you to. You might even want to ask when would be a good time to touch base again. But remember, the squeaky wheel only gets the oil as long as it's useful; it gets thrown out if it doesn't serve a purpose.

FOLLOW-UP CALLS TO HIRING MANAGERS

If you said you were going to follow up with a call—do it—unless you have been notified not to do so. Some people find follow up calls to be awkward and don't want to look like they are a pest or begging for a job. Both are good points. You don't want to be a pest or beg for a job, but you do want to stay at the top of the Hiring Manager's mind until he makes a hiring decision.

Make sure your call is relevant and that it will enhance your candidacy for the job. After you make the call, follow up with a quick e-mail with your contact information and a *very* short, "Thanks again."

These calls should be short and sweet, unless the Hiring Manager turns it into another interview and is seeking more information about your background and experience. Let them take the lead on extending the length of the call. Otherwise, you should end the call in no more than four to five minutes.

Act Like a Part of the Team in Follow Up—Show How You Can Be a Valuable Asset and Not a Pest

Again, put yourself in the Hiring Manager's shoes: If you are the busy Hiring Manager, what do you want from candidates—pesky interruptions, frequent calls and e-mails "begging" for information or further consideration? No! What the Hiring Managers wants, and more importantly needs, is to know you are still interested, how you can be of value and time to make a decision to find someone who is a problem solver and not a problem.

FOLLOW-UP EVEN IF YOU ARE NOT THE ONE HIRED

If you get a call letting you know that someone else has been selected— consider yourself lucky! Unfortunately, most companies are not good about showing the courtesy they expect *from* candidates *to* the candidates when it comes to delivering the bad news that they didn't get the job.

However you find out that you are not the chosen candidate, one last follow-up is not only appropriate, it is smart. It shows again your professionalism, interest in the company (not just in yourself), and helps remind the Hiring Manager to consider you for any future openings. Whether you can get the Hiring Manager on the phone (unlikely) or you follow-up in writing, the content of your message is the same.

Sample Follow-Up Letter Content When Not Chosen

- Thank the interviewer for the opportunity to meet with him.

- Express disappointment at not being chosen and wish the person who got the offer well.

- Let the Hiring Manager know you are still interested in them and their company and that you are interested in being considered in the future for other opportunities.

- Thank them for the professionalism and courtesy you were shown during the interview process.

- Ask for suggestions that might improve your candidacy in the future and referrals to others you might be able to network within your job search.

Summary

Each time you make contact or interview with a Hiring Manager, you have an opportunity to follow up and stay in contact with him to stay at the top of his mind and hopefully, at the top of his candidate list.

Make Meaningful Follow Up Connections With Hiring Managers

- Send a thank you letter within twenty-four hours to say thank you to each interviewer. Customize the note to each interviewer, referencing something you discussed.

- Take the opportunity to reaffirm your potential value to the company.

- Call within a week to ten days to follow up on the interview process and see if you can offer any other information to assist in the process.

- Continue to follow up until you know the job is filled or are told to stop contacting the Hiring Manager. This is kind of like walking a tight rope. The squeaky wheel gets the oil, but you don't want to annoy or be a pest. Let the Hiring Manager know you want to stay in touch and always ask what kind of follow up is appropriate.

- Always do what you say you will do. Call, send requested information, or follow up as promised or directed—on time, concisely and briefly.

Follow-Up Even If You Don't Get the Job

- Stay connected with the Hiring Manager—he is a good network prospect.

- Let him know you are disappointed, but would be open to being considered again in the future.

- Let him know there are no hard feelings and that you value getting to know him and would like to stay in touch.

NEGOTIATE A WIN-WIN-WIN COMPENSATION PACKAGE

Success Story

Susan was a successful executive with more than fifteen years of senior level responsibilities at a large computer company. When she was approached by a fast growing, innovative, smaller technology company, she was intrigued, even though she was happy where she was. She was itching for something more "fun."

Since her base salary and bonus were substantial in her current position, she really didn't think the smaller company would be able to structure a deal that could seriously interest her. But, she was interested in the job enough to interview and to prepare herself wisely to evaluate any potential offer. That's when she studied up on the *Negotiate a Win-Win-Win Compensation Package* secret. She was glad she did because it gave her a much broader perspective on how to negotiate an offer and what to consider. Here's what happened:

First, she *loved* the company and all the people she met. She was also blown away with the products under development. This little company was poised to make a huge splash in the consumer technology market and grow at an exponential rate.

Second, the company is located in a wonderful city where she had visited often and already had a number of good friends.

Third, was her biggest concern—could they offer her a compensation package that could replace what she would lose when she left her current employer? She had retirement, stock options, several other good benefits and a very competitive salary and bonus. She was hopeful, yet doubtful.

The Hiring Manager liked her also and they started to seriously discuss an offer. Susan referred back to what she had learned about negotiating a compensation package and found that there were lots of things to negotiate she had not originally considered.

She asked for, and they were willing to give her, a signing bonus that compensated for two years of potential lost bonus at her current job. She would have a company car, and best of all, she was offered a large stock option grant that more than made up for the options she was losing and then some. She was also fully vested in her current retirement plan and would not have to abandon it.

She was also offered a very competitive base salary, although not as much as her current base. The potential for her annual bonus, based on performance, was very attractive, however. She would also have a company paid cell phone and a number of other company paid perquisites that she was currently paying for herself.

The small company had many amenities that her current company didn't. They had a fitness and wellness center on site. She wouldn't have that expense any longer. She is now also encouraged to serve on a community board, that is near and dear to her heart, on company time.

Probably most importantly, she asked that she would be guaranteed two additional staff members if she was able to reach aggressive, specific, and predetermined company performance goals. They agreed!

It was a win-win-win!

Remember: when a candidate receives a job offer, there are two things they may not be aware of: 1) that you can negotiate the offer, and 2) what parts of the offer are negotiable. The above success story shows you that just about everything is negotiable as long as it benefits all involved. See for yourself how easy negotiating an offer can be when you know how to do it.

WHAT'S IN A JOB OFFER

Okay, let's say you've impressed your networking contact and got the introduction to the Hiring Manager in the company you're interested in. Then you proceeded to:

- Target the needs of that company, dead on, in your customized résumé and cover letter.

- Ace your interview and match your qualifications to the needs of the Hiring Manager and the company, and show him how hiring you will help solve his problems.

- Follow-up without being overbearing and kept yourself at the top of the Hiring Manager's mind throughout the hiring process.

- And then you were offered the job!

Now comes the time to work through your compensation package. We're assuming you've done everything else right, so there should be no horrendous surprises at this point and your job search should come to a successful, mutually beneficial conclusion.

Hiring Managers' Comments Regarding Negotiating an Offer

"A bit of give and take is fine. It is about clear and candid communication with concerns expressed. Ultimatums and absolutes will quickly curtail the conversation."

"Don't play games. Groundwork should have been done before. Job seekers should be specific with needs and wants."

"I think it is important to have some negotiation around the total rewards. The tone should be that of being confident that you are worth an 'expected' amount. Often, you may need to come in at a level below this, but your acceptance should be prefaced with a statement like 'I am willing to start at this, because I'm confident that I will be able to demonstrate my value to the organization and work up to the amount I believe I should be at.'"

"When people bring logical or fact based issues, we try to work with them and solve the gap. If it's just pure negotiation for the sake of it, it's off-putting. People, who negotiate too hard, without good reason, often don't last long."

The bottom line in all negotiations is to:

- Know what you are worth, what the market will bear, what the company can afford and what others are making for related work in the same industry and in the same geographic region.

- Know what's important to you. The job is more than salary, so know what else is important to you that you should consider.

When You Are the Chosen Candidate

Almost all job offers come by telephone, so it is imperative that your telephone be covered day and night! In a tight job market, when there are many qualified candidates, some companies will just go to the next qualified candidate, if they have to work too hard to contact you. You certainly don't want to miss out on your dream job because you were out walking the dog!

It Is Essential That You Have

Your cell phone—Your cell phone may be the best option for the phone number on all your job marketing materials. Be sure your phone is charged, you can get a clear signal, you have it turned on, and you have it with you. Check for messages frequently.

Set up your phones with a professional voice mail recording. Give the Hiring Manager your cell phone— you don't want to miss that important call!

Someone at home—A member of your family, preferably an adult, is home at all times. If a child is the message carrier, be sure they are prepared and able to get the message accurately.

Voice mail recorder—You need to have a reliable phone message service, either with your phone service provider or a machine you have purchased. The message should be professional, short and checked often when you are not home to receive messages. The message should be your voice and *no goofy messages*. Be sure the recording capability for each message is long enough for the caller to leave a complete message.

Telephone Answering Service—As a last choice, arrange for a professional answering service. This might be an excessive expense, however.

The Objective of Any Negotiation

Your objective, in your job offer negotiation, is the same as any negotiation; make a mutually beneficial deal for both sides. Pushing too hard from either side leaves a bad taste in one's mouth (or both mouths), so look for what can make you both happy. If done honestly, with supporting facts, logic, and integrity, both of you are approaching the negotiation process from the same standpoint—to arrive at a mutually beneficial agreement.

Negotiating a job offer can open the door wide for current or future opportunity or it can shut the door if it is not mutually beneficial to all concerned.

KNOW WHAT YOU CAN AND SHOULD NEGOTIATE FOR

Understand it is not *only* about cash. Consider the company's entire compensation package. And remember to:

- Keep issues on the table that are important to your satisfaction.

- Know what you bring to the job that differentiates you from your competition.

- Establish your decision criteria in advance. Know what you will accept and what you won't.

- Be willing to compromise on lesser important issues.

- Be willing and prepared to politely stand firm for very important issues.

- Recognize what lies in between as open to negotiation.

- Accept, without overdue worry, what you may have "left on the table."

What is Included in a Typical Offer

- Job description and title
- Start date
- Base salary
- Bonus (if a bonus eligible job)
- Insurance and pension
- Vacation
- Reporting relationship to boss
- Department and team
- Relocation expenses
- Stock options (if the position is eligible)

There is usually much more to an offer, but most written offers will have some combination of the items above and may have supplemental documents explaining them further.

WHAT IS NEGOTIABLE IN AN OFFER

Actually, most anything is negotiable—within reason. You certainly don't want to negotiate everything, however. It is also most desirable to try to get your offer in writing, if possible. Some things to consider when reviewing an offer are:

- Large companies may have highly structured compensation plans, benefits, and titles, but they also may have many more things in an offer, as they probably have greater resources. They need to make your offer fair for what they are asking you to do, yet one that won't create inequities or inconsistencies with people already working for the company as well.

- Small companies may offer fewer benefits and amenities, may have greater flexibility, but may have fewer resources.

- Non-profits are usually most strapped for resources, but individuals who are working in the non-profit sector of the job market are usually highly motivated by the work they are doing and willing to compromise on compensation. Non-profits are more able to "compensate" through psychic rewards, use of their facilities, free admissions to their performances, etc.

- Most companies have seventy to eighty percent of compensation in base salary and twenty to thirty percent in other benefits and perquisites—the perks.

- In bonus eligible positions, bonuses are usually in addition to other benefits and perks.

There Are Generally Four Categories To Consider With Most Job Offers

1. **The Job Itself.** The level and scope of responsibility, number of direct reports, title, and decision-making authority are all issues that should have been discussed and decided in the interview process. Review an offer to insure what you thought you were hiring on for is what is in writing or in the verbal offer.

   Resources available to you such as budget, temporary help, space, equipment, location of office, work schedule and the option of working from home should also have been decided in the interview process.

   Some companies also offer employment contracts, which usually have a guarantee of a length of time you will be employed, what you will be doing, and spells out what might happen if things don't work out before the end of the contract. Consult an employment attorney before accepting or signing an employment contract.

2. **Cash.** There are two major types of cash compensation: *base salary*, which is what you can get the most information about on the internet for the level, title, and scope of the job. The second type of cash compensation is often called *"at risk" compensation*. That means that it usually isn't guaranteed and that it is tied to your direct performance, the performance of your team or division, and the overall performance of the company, or some combination of these. This can come in the form of a cash bonus (sign on bonuses are in this category, also) project bonuses, commissions, special incentives, etc.

3. **Benefits that Cost the Company Cash.** Vacations, insurances, relocation expenses, third party equity buy-out of real estate, pension, non-qualified flexible retirement investments, 401Ks, savings and profit sharing plans, stock options, phantom stock, company car and expenses are included in this. Tread carefully, if these have not been included in your offer. Unless you have had these benefits with other companies and in similar positions, it could be considered presumptive on your part to bring them up. Do your *homework* before asking!

4. **Benefits That May Not Have Direct Additional Costs To The Company.** These benefits could include: time and support for you to volunteer in the community, community organization board memberships, employee event planning and participation (employee clubs), employee discount programs, discounts on company products or services.

HOW SHOULD YOU STRATEGIZE YOUR NEGOTIATIONS

Negotiate only what is important to you and a few things that are "negotiable." Know which is which. Focus on the former. Choose your battles and be reasonable and fact based. Leave emotion and personality out of it.

Here is a suggested order to negotiate the offer: First, address issues that affect the position right now—when the offer is made. Next, negotiate for the future—early performance and salary review, guaranteed bonus in twelve months, etc.

Don't Knock Yourself Out of the Running with Blunders

Six "Knock-out" negotiation tactics to avoid (and by knock-out we mean they will knock you out of the running faster than butter melts in an open fire):

1. **Poor research and lack of preparation**. In today's internet world and with good networking, there's no excuse for the job seeker not to know his worth in the marketplace and what a company may be able to offer as a compensation package.

2. **Bringing up salary too soon in the hiring process.** A new (but very true) adage says, "He who blinks first loses and the person with the most patience has the most power." If you can, get the offer before beginning to discuss salary. Then, you can be more specific about salary and all benefits included in the compensation package. Asking too early may force you to reveal the salary you'd accept. That's bad. It might also indicate to the Hiring Manager that you are too focused on the money and not enough on the company. That's even worse.

3. **Not negotiating at all.** If you settle for less than what you need or know you are worth, just settling for what you're offered, could be your worst mistake. Having said that, don't negotiate just for the sake of negotiating. If it's an *outstanding* offer, you know it and so does the Hiring Manager. Ask for a short time to thoroughly review the offer and then take it graciously, with enthusiasm, and gratitude—but not groveling.

4. **Accepting an offer that will make you unhappy.** Most offers do give you an opportunity to refine and negotiate a bit. You may dislike the negotiation process or feel uncomfortable about negotiating, but settling does more harm. Consider this: your raises (based on percent of salary) will be smaller, pension contributions (based on percent of your salary) will be smaller and emotionally, the decision to accept less than you think you are worth can make you feel cheated and unhappy with your work, boss and the company.

5. **Accepting/declining a job offer too quickly.** Remember what we said about the person who has the most patience has the most power, well that's doubly true about accepting or declining a job offer. Don't move in either direction too quickly, no matter how long you have been waiting, because it's at the point of receiving a job offer that you have the most power. The Hiring Manager has chosen you, so use that power appropriately for your benefit. Ask for at least twenty-four to forty-eight hours to review what's good or lacking in the offer before accepting or rejecting it outright. Most companies are willing to give you some time to think about the offer, so take advantage of it. And remember, you should be able to negotiate various elements of the offer to make a good one even better and a poor one very acceptable.

6. **Asking for unrealistic changes in a counteroffer.** Do propose one or two changes that are based in facts and are really important to you, but do not make changes to every element in the offer. Your motto should be: choose your battles wisely, if you really want the job.

Throughout the negotiation process, it is critical that you are positive, enthusiastic and realistic. Be sure the Hiring Manager knows you want the job and that you appreciate the offer. Don't nit-pick and don't be inflexible—you probably won't get everything you ask for. Stay focused on what is most important to you; and consider the entire package—*everything* has some value.

It's Win-Win-Win Situation

Before you close off your negotiations, be sure you have accomplished the most benefit for all concerned. This is not like buying a car in which you want to make sure you better the other guy. You're about to begin, what hopefully will be, a long and profitable relationship. And it must be good for everyone involved—the company, the Hiring Manager and yourself. Make it not only a win-win-win situation, but also a winning beginning.

Summary

You have the offer, now you need to evaluate it and decide what to negotiate. Your goal is an offer that you, the Hiring Manager and the company can all feel good about.

When you are the chosen candidate:

- It is critical that you are prepared to get the offer. That means insuring you are reachable.

- You need to insure the message gets through to you. One of the following methods is essential or a combination of them. Use your cell phone, be sure someone is home to accept calls, have an effective voice mail recorder or hire a professional answering service.

What is negotiable in an offer?

- Know the advantages and constraints of large, small and non-profit companies.

- Most anything is negotiable, but negotiating is an art and should be done with facts and reason.

- The job itself can be negotiated to some extent, but most of this should have been discovered during the interview process.

- Cash is the most common point of negotiation.

- Benefits that cost cash are also common negotiation points.

- Benefits that may not have direct additional costs to the company are often executive level negotiation points, but may have some relevance to middle managers and others as well.

How should you strategize your negotiation?

- Start with the current situation and then move to future, if that doesn't work.

- Start with cash, then at risk cash, then benefits, then other items.

Avoid these blunders in the negotiation process:

- Be sure your research is accurate and up to date.

- Let the company make the offer first. Try not to bring up salary first. Let them.

- Not negotiating at all may put you at a disadvantage long term.

- Accepting or turning down an offer on the spot can also put you at a long-term disadvantage.

- Being too aggressive, unrealistic, emotional, or stubborn can quickly kill an offer. You look like future trouble, and no Hiring Manager needs that!

Visit www.TheCareerSuite.com/20dosanddonts to download your free, *The 20 most important things you should do to land the job you want and the 20 things you should absolutely avoid.* These twenty dos and don'ts are based on all the information we provided in this book. In other words, the do's and don'ts for each stage of your job search—to help you land the job you want quickly and with less stress.

You'll also find additional valuable free information and tips on our website on how to outshine your competition in your job search—and win the job you want now. Visit us soon and often!

JOB FIT—A MUTUAL ATTRACTION IN A SUCCESSFUL JOB SEARCH

Picture this: you're trying to jam a size twelve into a size ten running shoe. Ouch! Or this: trying on a gorgeous diamond ring that is two sizes too large. Even if you do get it on, there's a big chance you will lose it—kind of like a job that's too big or a bad fit. Then there's the old saying, "You can't put a square peg in a round hole."

The same is true when it comes to perfectly matching your needs with a prospective employer's needs. And we're not just talking about the needs of the job itself—the skills, experience and knowledge you need to fulfill the company's needs. It's important that you consider the company's culture, environment, policies and procedures to ensure a good fit.

So What Really Makes a Good "Fit"

There isn't one definitive answer to this question, but many companies tend to look at four things:

1. How you **think and reason.**

2. Identifying your **occupational interests.**

3. Your **behavior** in business situations.

4. Your **adaptability** to their unique organizational culture.

As we mentioned before, many companies are attempting to mitigate "gut feeling" hiring practices around the first three issues of fit by using validated pre-employment assessments. Most of us don't relish taking these assessments, but if you are asked to do so, just relax and be honest in your responses. Frankly, these assessments can spare you and the company a lot of future pain, if they determine you might not be the best candidate for their position. That doesn't feel very good at the time, if you don't get the job offer, but this fact has been proven *many* times.

Hiring Managers do everything they can to try to make good hiring decisions for their company and for you. You also have some responsibility to assess your own fit for jobs you apply for. So, what can you do to make a good assessment of your fit for a job opening? Knowing yourself, what you do well, and what keeps you engaged in your work is a good place to begin assessing your fit. As you think through these issues, make a **Personal Career Needs** list that you can refer to when considering job openings.

What Hiring Managers Said About the Job Seeker's Fit With Their Organizations

"Fit is critical, not just something nice. When attempting to strengthen and perpetuate a strong culture, you need a diversity of people, but ones with similar values and fit. We interview the heck out of people and make sure lots of people have the opportunity to meet candidates. How someone comports themselves with everyone is vital. We check with everyone who comes in contact with the job seeker from the CEO to the administrative person to the chauffer from the airport limo company."

"Fit is important, but does not mandate one personality type. Fit is more about values and outlook on life."

"Fit is vital. I look for indications of advancement, accepting the business's mission and pride in their work."

"The chemistry among workers is paramount. Additionally, the job seeker must naturally embrace the culture of the organization."

"Fit is an individual who can enhance and improve an organization. Fit is not someone who can come in and change the world."

"Fit is best seen in a job seeker's "soft skills" such as listening, kindness, long-standing personal relationships, and not critical of their last boss, company, or position as well as his problem-solving and communication skills."

As we mentioned, doing an honest job of self-assessment of fit can spare you and the company from future pain. Where there is a good fit, there is good performance. Where the fit is not so good, the performance is often the same. No company likes to dismiss employees for not doing well. You don't need a short-term job on your future résumé, and you don't want to be back in the job market any time soon.

As you read this secret on "fit," it may appear that "it's all about you," which is going against our premise that a job search is "all about the Hiring Manager and his company." Don't be mistaken; we haven't changed our point of view.

"Fit" is more than just being well qualified for the job you want, it also means fitting into an organization's culture and being comfortable with their policies and procedures, etc. Think long-term about fit and don't make a short-term decision. The Hiring Manager won't.

Doing a good job of assessing what you need from a job is definitely addressing your needs, but it also meets the needs of the Hiring Manager to have a candidate who has done their homework, knows what they have to offer, and how the job will enthuse and engage them in the work. That's really thinking like the Hiring Manager because that's what he needs and is looking for in a new employee.

The Society for Human Resource Management (SHRM) conducted a survey of over six hundred employees in the United States to determine what was important to them in a job. The list below shows the percentage of people who rated certain items "very important."

Surveys like these have been done at least every ten years, since the end of World War II, by different organizations and agencies. Job security, pay, benefits, and recognition for accomplishments have *always* been in the top ten. In times of economic hardship, *job security, pay, and benefits* tend to be at the top of the list. When times are easier, *recognition* pops to the top of the list. Take a look at the list and see how you would rank these job factors for yourself and add the top ranked ones to your ***Personal Career Needs*** list.

63% Job security
60% Benefits
57% Compensation/pay
55% Opportunity to use skills/abilities
54% Feeling safe in the work environment
52% Relationship with the immediate supervisor
52% Management recognition of employee job performance
51% Communication between employees and senior management
50% The work itself
47% Autonomy and independence
46% Flexibility to balance life and work issues
45% Meaningfulness of job
45% Overall corporate culture
42% Relationships with co-workers
39% Contribution of work to organization's business goals
35% Job-specific training
34% Variety of work
32% Career advancement opportunities
31% Organization's commitment to corporate social responsibility
30% Organization's commitment to professional development
29% Paid training and tuition reimbursement programs
22% Career development opportunities
17% Organization's commitment to a "green" workplace

Some Things To Consider Before You Decide To Apply for a Job Opening

- **Can I do the job?** Does your background and experience fit with the requirements of the job? Be ambitious, but realistic. Use your time wisely in pursuit of jobs where you will be a likely candidate.

- **Does this work interest me?** Do the mission, values and business of the company engage you? It is a proven fact that people are more successful when they are doing something they like to do.

- **What will this job do for my career and personal aspirations?** Will this job potentially contribute to the kind of career and life you have envisioned for yourself? For your family?

- **Will the work environment fit my needs?** Does the amount of travel, the pay and benefits, commute, and work schedule fit for you? Is it in an office or plant? Indoors or outdoors? Will you be an individual contributor or a member of a team? Are you willing to do what it will take to be successful?

Your goal is not to be considered for any or every job, but to be a strong candidate for the *right* job for you. Assessing your own needs and interests up front will save you and the Hiring Manager a lot of time and energy.

Congratulations! You Are the Chosen Candidate and Have an Offer

You've got the offer. Do you want it? Don't panic and accept the first offer out of desperation. Now is when you need to go back to your ***Personal Career Needs*** list and see if the job is a good fit from your point of view. Making a poor decision at this point may affect your long-term career success, your personal satisfaction and even health.

Do a good job of assessing your own fit for a job and you'll know when the job is right or if you should walk away. If you decide to walk away, do it for the right reason and with confidence that another offer may be a better one for you.

CULTURAL FIT—WHAT MAKES YOUR PROSPECTIVE COMPANY "TICK"

You'll also need to discover what you can about the company's culture. Check that your personal work values match company culture. Recognize that it's not just the work that impacts your success, it's also the environment that brings satisfaction or misery. Discover what employees like best and least about working there.

Blogging and social media can help you demonstrate what makes you a great "cultural fit" for the job you want.

Here's where blogging and social media can be of use. Use these to demonstrate what makes you a great "cultural fit." Incorporate examples that show your cultural competencies such as: teamwork, flexibility, leadership, etc. They are a great means to show your sincere interest and enthusiasm for a position. But remember, to keep everything professional!

The Importance of Being Fit for a Job

Poor fit is #1 reason for failure in most employment situations. So, do not minimize the importance of how you fit when developing your marketing plan for your job search. The right job must be right for you—*and the company*—to be a great fit. It's a business marriage that will last as long as it remains mutually beneficial to all parties involved.

The right job must be right for everyone involved because a poor fit can cost everyone.

As you'll see, the right fit is critical to the Hiring Manager. That's because even if someone is competent and qualified to do a job, mismatches or a poor fit is followed by terminations that are costly. Such premature terminations can cost from fifty to one hundred fifty percent of the annual salary, according to HR Consultancy Saratoga Institute, a consulting service of PricewaterhouseCoopers.

Nearly, one in three newly hired employees leave voluntarily or involuntarily before the end of their first year. And, according to Saratoga, this number has been increasing steadily for the last four years. And consider the fact that after a mismatched person leaves, the Hiring Manager has to go through the hiring process again, including all costs associated with it.

Research Is Key

As in every previous aspect of your job search, as well as those yet to come, research is the key to a job seeker's success when it comes to being fit for a job. Research how a prospective company's goals and yours can work together. For instance, what are the vision, goals and objectives of the company? Where may the company's goals take it and, in turn, take you as an employee? Consider whether that's a satisfactory direction for you. Can you and the company walk the walk together that accomplishes those goals?

This is not the time you want to be the square peg in a round hole or vice versa. Consider, thoroughly, what the company expects from you. Consider, thoroughly, what you can expect from the company. Take in the full picture. The Hiring Manager will do the same.

Mismatched Candidates and Jobs Are Costly Mistakes

Harvard Business Review published the results of a study of over 350,000 employed people. The goal of the study was to determine the effectiveness and validity of common hiring practices. The study showed that men and women perform at the same level, age had no bearing on ability to perform and ethnicity didn't affect performance. The conclusions reached? It's not experience that counts, or college degrees or other accepted factors—success hinges on intangibles such as whether the hired person's personality fit with the job culture.

A Poor Cultural Fit Drains Organizational Effectiveness, Kills Employee Morale and Hampers Creativity

That's why a number of organizations have become more flexible with regard to credentials than with fit. In other words, the person who fits in and who has lighter weight credentials than someone who may not fit in, may very well be the candidate the Hiring Manager chooses. Costly mismatch mistakes are also why so many companies are using validated, pre-employment testing to try and determine fit.

A Hiring Manager considers your accomplishments, talent, experience and how you handle yourself during and after interviews. They also look at how you interact with employees not involved in the interview process, such as the receptionist, administrative assistants, guards, and other front line employees. They note how your personality and work habits might mesh with people you would work with. So, be at your best from the moment you leave your home in the morning until you return that evening!

It's obvious, then, that fit is much more than your accomplishments and experience. It is really more about values and outlook on life. It's about job seekers who are well grounded and share the organization's essential values.

And remember what one Hiring Manager said that sums up the interview:

> *"The Hiring Manager must be able to see the individual in his company and in the prospective position and it's the job seeker's role to help him do just that."*

OTHER METHODS OF JOB SEARCH TO CONSIDER

W e saw that seventy to ninety percent of all jobs are in the "hidden job market" and are usually found by networking. What about the remaining ten to thirty percent of the jobs and what methods can you use to search for them? Here are a few options you may want to consider:

Consider all your options. Choose what fits together most effectively in your job search marketing plan; then consistently work your plan!

- Respond to advertisements and Internet job postings.

- Search out recruiting and executive search firms.

- Apply at staffing and temporary agencies.

- Find local work at job fairs.

- Cold call or walk-in to a company that interests you.

- Mass email or direct mail distribution résumés.

Some things to consider about each of these methods follow.

RESPONDING TO ADVERTISEMENTS AND INTERNET JOB POSTINGS

Unfortunately, what many people find when responding to ads and Internet postings is that only about a third of them actually represent a real job opening. Companies, staffing firms, and others sometimes run ads whether they are hiring or not. Their reasons vary, but some do this to have a steady flow of applicants for jobs they hire into frequently, some are required by law or company policy to advertise before filling the job with a job seeker they have already selected.

RECRUITING AND EXECUTIVE SEARCH FIRMS

There are two main types of recruiting and search firms: *retained* and *contingent*. A retained recruiter or search firm is employed by the Hiring Manager and company to find the "perfect" candidate. They are paid up front, usually a third at the beginning of the project, a third when they present their first candidates, and the balance about ninety days into the project or when the project is terminated—sometimes with no hire! They get paid—no matter the outcome.

Many **retained** search firms choose not to accept unsolicited résumés from job seekers, and few to none will represent the job seeker in the job market and look for a job for them. So, calling them and asking them to represent you will probably result in a "no." These recruiters, sometimes called "headhunters," typically are hired to find senior level job seekers who will earn in excess of $100,000 a year plus bonus. The firm's fee is usually based on twenty-five to thirty-five percent of the successful hire's first year cash compensation.

Contingent recruiters will selectively represent job seekers. If you call them and have the skills and background that they think they can place, they may choose to present you to a Hiring Manager and company they believe will be a good match for you. (This doesn't mean you can hire them to find you a job, however. The company doing the hiring pays them.) They typically find good candidates and then try to find a company who needs them. They are paid only when they make a placement, so they work very hard to make a good match with the Hiring Manager and company—sometimes too hard because their fee depends on it. Even if they present good candidates and there are open jobs, if no one gets hired, they don't get paid.

Some other good things about retained and contingent firms. With the job market as tight as it is, many Hiring Managers and companies have laid-off their recruiting staff and are turning to these firms for assistance, so they may be more linked into the company needs than they may have been traditionally.

Many of these firms specialize in certain industries or have specific recruiters who do. They often have strong and trusted relationships with Hiring Managers and companies. If you are working with a recruiter or search firm, be sure they are well connected into the industry of your choice.

Some headhunters and recruiters have outstanding reputations and ethics. Unfortunately, a few do not. Be selective in who you work with. Bad recruiter behavior can reflect poorly on you as well. We would also generally advise against paying a recruiter to represent you. No one can really guarantee to find you a job that meets your needs and that of a Hiring Manager and company, so you generally are better off representing yourself and save your money rather than work with a poor or unethical recruiter.

Note: Also beware of bait and switch recruiters who contact you with job opportunities, invite you to their office and then try to sell you other career products. Reputable recruiters don't ask you for money, they earn their fee from the Hiring Manager and company.

STAFFING, CONTRACT, AND TEMPORARY AGENCIES

Staffing and temporary agencies can be life savers to job seekers who have popular skills that companies need for limited periods of time. These temporary assignments can often lead to permanent ones also. The types of jobs that are particularly attractive to these agencies are administrative professionals, accounting, hospitality, payroll, information technologies, and others. Hiring Managers and companies sometimes outsource jobs to these types of agencies also.

JOB FAIRS

Job fairs can be somewhat similar to answering advertisements. Many companies are there to collect résumés for future needs (not a bad thing!). Job fairs can be a good opportunity to meet with Hiring Managers face to face and create other networking prospects with companies and other job seekers.

COLD CALLING OR WALK-IN

Generally speaking, cold calling and walk-in works for minimum wage jobs that experience high turnover—never for professionals or managers unless they are highly skilled, may have very specialized talents, and are patient and persistent. Most Hiring Managers won't make time for a cold call or walk-in—they don't have to.

MASS EMAIL OR DIRECT MAIL DISTRIBUTION RÉSUMÉ

Blanketing the world with your résumé or e-mail blasting it to people who don't know you are futile methods of job search in today's world. The only way it could have some pay off for you is if your résumé is sent with an introductory letter from someone the Hiring Manager knows. If you choose to send out lots of résumés to people you don't know, then the only way to make that pay off is to follow it up with a phone call. Generally speaking, save the stamps!

Most of these other methods of conducting a job search can be of some benefit and, combined with effective networking, can land you the job you are looking for.

ADDENDUM

As promised earlier, here are the fourteen questions we asked Hiring Managers in various industries all across the United States. Their responses, along with our forty plus years of human resource and marketing management, were the basis for the seven secrets found in this book. We hope you have found these secrets to be valuable to your job search success.

1. What does a candidate need to do to get a first interview? Do you have specific criteria a candidate must meet to get a first interview? If so, what are they?

2. In an applicant's first contact with you—by phone, email, personal referral, letter, or other means—what makes you interested in interviewing him or her?

3. Do you prepare specific interview questions when starting a series of interviews for a job? If so, how do you determine what questions to ask? Do you have any "favorite" interview questions? Why? What do the answers tell you?

4. *In addition to talent and experience*, what does a successful candidate need to demonstrate to convince you he or she could be an outstanding hire? How is he or she different from other candidates?

5. What expectations do you have of a candidate during an interview? Typically, how quickly can you determine if you want to take a candidate to the next step of the hiring process?

6. Do you have specific criteria a candidate must meet to get additional interviews? If so, what are they?

7. How important is their ability to "fit" your organization? How do you determine if a candidate will fit or not? What three to five behaviors/actions would indicate to you a candidate would fit in?

8. What kind of follow-up impresses you after an initial contact? After the first or subsequent interviews? What kind of follow-up annoys or disappoints you?

9. What are three to five automatic "knock-outs," "hot button" issues, or "deal breakers" a candidate should avoid? Why is each of these important? If a candidate shows any of these, is there anything he or she can do to overcome them? If so, what might they be? If not, why not?

10. When ready to make a final hiring decision, how much do you weigh each of the following before making that decision?

    _____% Company specific criteria

    _____% Data gathered from candidate before, during and after interviews (résumés, cover letters, email, etc.)

    _____% Intuition or "Gut instinct"

11. When working through a final compensation offer for and with a candidate, how much negotiation is enough? Too much? What behaviors/actions during negotiations by the candidate would impress you? Irritate you?

12. How concerned should a candidate be to work through the human resource people versus going straight to a Hiring Manager?

13. What advantages are there to a candidate if he or she is referred to you rather than responding to an ad or coming through a recruiter? Why?

14. What percent of your candidates come to you through:

      _____% Company solicited résumés (either advertised job opening, internal recruiter or other means originated by company)

      _____% Unsolicited résumés

      _____% External recruiter

      _____% Internal referral

      _____% External referral

INDEX

Symbols

5 different types of interviews, 91
5 step sales process, 44
7 Ps of marketing and selling, 35
75% and 90% of all available jobs, 73
ABCs of Follow up and Follow-thru, 101

A

ABC network poll, 14
Acceptance, 13
action steps, 9
a deep pit, xvii
AIDA, 41, 48, 49
all about the Hiring Manager, 123
Anger, 12

B

Blame, 12
brand, 37, 38, 39, 41, 42, 46, 48, 66, 90

C

Career Xroads, 75
change, 8, 10, 11, 13, 14, 15, 16, 17, 19, 20, 32, 36, 60, 122
children, 14, 24, 25
company's culture, 121, 126
compensation package, 44, 93, 109, 111, 115
confidence, 3, 9, 13, 18, 33, 47, 86
Conscious Competent, 36
control, 7, 12, 15, 18, 19, 21, 24
coping strategies, 17, 20
Corporate informa-tion.com, 34

courage, integrity, and conviction, 6
cover letter, 33, 35, 52, 54, 55, 64, 65, 66, 67, 69, 70, 82
customer, 33, 35, 36, 37, 47, 48, 61, 64, 98
customized resumes, 55

D

Denial/disbelief, 12
Discouragement or even depression, 12
dragon, 8
DunandBradstreet.com, 34

E

economy, 1, 17, 20
ERMA, 23, 27
expectations, 17, 133
expenses, 23, 24, 25, 27, 112, 114

F

family, i, xviii, 13, 14, 15, 16, 18, 19, 21, 22, 23, 24, 25, 26, 27, 85, 110, 125
financial action plan, 25, 27
financial plans, 14, 15
Financial Review, 22
find a new job, 14, 22, 27
fit, ii, 43, 52, 53, 54, 63, 65, 87, 92, 102, 121, 122, 123, 124, 125, 126, 127, 128, 134
follow-up strategy and tactics, 99
follow up with a call, 103

G

Google.com, 34

IF YOU'RE A FAN OF THIS BOOK, PLEASE TELL OTHERS...

- Write about *Win the Job You Want!* on your blog, Twitter, MySpace, and Facebook page.
- Suggest *Win the Job You Want!* to friends.
- When you're in a bookstore, ask them if they carry the book. The book is available through all major distributors, so any bookstore that does not have *Win the Job You Want!* in stock, can easily order it.
- Write a positive review of *Win the Job You Want!* on www.amazon.com.
- Send my publisher, HigherLife Publishing, suggestions on Web sites, conferences, and events you know of where this book could be offered at media@ahigherlife.com.
- Purchase additional copies to give away as gifts.

CONNECT WITH US...

To learn more about *Win the Job You Want,* please contact us at:

Pat Andrew
Andrew-Hill LLC
pandrew@TheCareerSuite.com

Eleanor A. Hill
Andrew-Hill LLC
eahill@TheCareerSuite.com

ARE YOU READY TO WIN THE JOB YOU WANT?

We're here to help. Check out our website **www.TheCareerSuite.com** for tons of free resources, and downloadable and online coaching opportunities that can help make you the standout job candidate for any Hiring Manager.